A History of Magic Bus

Every Day You'll See The Dust

A History of Magic Bus

Incomplete and Unverified

****

Researched and Compiled by
Richard Gregory

****

With photographs from
the Magic Bus archive

****

Samizdata Publications

Every Day You'll See The Dust
A History of Magic Bus

by

Richard Gregory

First Edition 2025

ISBN 9781068244902

© Richard Gregory 2025
All Rights Reserved
The moral right of the author has been asserted
Unauthorised duplication contravenes applicable laws
Use by generative artificial intelligence technology
for any purpose is expressly prohibited

All photographs
© Magic Bus Archive
or public domain
except where stated

Design by Richard Gregory

Published by
Samizdata Publications
16 Carthew Villas
London W6 0BS

Printed in England
by Imprint Digital

For Cornelia & Barrie

Foreword

Memory - how fickle!

Richard Gregory has set down in this book many long forgotten facts (some unknown to me) about the Magic Bus company, of which, along with Greg Williams, I was a co-founder.

In a sympathetic way Richard has assembled vignettes from many who experienced the same events that I did, and it is fascinating to read of those events as seen through different eyes.

Graham Paton's story, for example, describes our shared trip from Kabul in early 1972, through the Kabul Gorge and the Khyber Pass, to Lahore in Pakistan. The war between India and Pakistan was over, but the land border between them was still closed.

Kabul at the time was thick with restless hippies who were stalled in their journeys to India and Nepal. But we found a way to get some of them to India: we booked 40 seats on a Swissair flight from Karachi to Bombay. Both India and Pakistan had money in Swiss banks, and they allowed Swissair to fly over their airspace. We undertook to drive a full busload of passengers from Kabul to Karachi to catch the flight.

Graham Paton describes one of our bus passengers as a *"daughter of the Raj"*, an English lady who *"might have been sixty"*. I remember her as a Scottish nurse, aged 76, who said she had made her first journey to India twenty-five years earlier, and that in those days it had been *"somewhat of an adventure"*.

Graham also recalled problems with the bus radiator, but he did not know the back story. After we left London in December 1971 the radiator had repeatedly been assaulted by the fan, which broke due to 'metal fatigue'. Matters came to a head in northern Iran - the area was suffering its coldest winter for thirty years - when the fan flew off its mounting and punctured the radiator.

The cold weather was so extreme that Greg Williams and his co-driver David Hurd used flaming rag torches to thaw out the fuel lines in the morning before setting off. Fortunately diesel doesn't explode like petrol does!

In Kabul we found a wizard who cut out the center portion of the radiator, installed a smaller one in the hole, and welded up pipes to circulate the water between the parts. It worked up to a point.

I remember the roller-coaster ride down the Kabul Gorge, the balmy lush green plain of Jalalabad (a joy after that harsh winter) and the climb through the hairpin turns of the Khyber Pass.

I like Graham Paton's description of slinging around each hairpin (remember that the front wheels on the bus are behind the driver) and sleeping outside under the moonlight. I remember that night seeing ghostly figures on bicycles, wrapped in blankets against the chill, and water buffalo plodding along with carts carrying giant loads of green grass, plying the side of the road.

As we drove, the occasional oncoming vehicles flashed their lights on and off so you could get an idea of how big they were (there were no street lights and the road was one-lane wide). The vehicles would do a strange *'do-si-do'* upon meeting up, to slant off the road just-so, simultaneously, and to pass each other in a whoosh, sometimes so close as to knock the wing mirrors awry.

Whatever else he was, Greg Williams was a very good driver.

At Peshawar the radiator had begun to leak badly, so we asked the passengers to chew gum and applied the wads. No good. We tried putting in raw eggs. Nothing doing. Then we tried porridge oats, and that worked to slow the flow. I was the one who fed the horseless carriage one handful of oats and one jug of water every half hour, into a funnel in a hole we cut in the dashboard, through a hose to the radiator. I was less concerned with chillums than with my heroics in keeping the radiator from running dry.

I was pretty tired when we reached Lahore. Graham Paton says we got a police escort into the city to protect us from the unfriendly crowds, but I have no memory of it. I do recall that we changed drivers in Lahore, so I didn't go to Karachi myself, but I heard that the bus just made it to the flight, and the passengers had to run in a herd across the tarmac to get on board.

We made it back to Kabul and tried to pull off the same stunt with Swissair a second time, but we were a day late and Spacey Pete stole all the passengers in his green double decker bus.

So we drove the Morris van that Greg had left in Kabul to Peshawar, where we had it transformed into what is remembered as 'the original Magic Bus', featured on the front cover of this book.

****

Now that I have passed my 76th year I would say that - like the elderly lady on the bus - our era was *"somewhat of an adventure"*, a time which, in this era, seems fantastical and free.

I am indebted to Richard Gregory, who I first met in London just a month ago, for researching and compiling this book. It is a story that has waited to be told for forty years, and he has done it!

I am grateful also to Barrie Moreton, a true intrepid, who had kept Greg's papers since his death and by chance met up with Richard and gave him access. I am very pleased that Barrie telephoned me after 35 years since I had last seen him, and asked me to contribute my memories. I'm glad I kept my landline!

Other pivotal characters have passed away, been uncontactable, or declined to add their memories for reasons of their own. But they were all part of the history of Magic Bus.

Cornelia Gaines Olsen (Nee)
Connecticut, October 2025

Preface

In summer 1974, at the age of 18, I bought a one-way bus ticket to Kathmandu to take part in what the US media called the Hashish Trail and the UK media subsequently called the Hippie Trail.

Magic Bus, which later become synonymous with the trip, had yet to make its presence felt and I was unaware of it.

Over the next few years my travels took me to Holland, Greece, Morocco and Goa, but fate decreed that I would never set foot on a Magic Bus myself, though I remember the company advertising regularly in the newspapers.

I began to write about my youthful adventures in 2005, and that led to my extensive research into the Hippie Trail phenomenon, which Magic Bus was certainly a part of. But information about the company was surprisingly hard to find.

So this book partly exists to address that historical deficit, because there is an interesting story to be told about a company that was once a household name for young people across Europe.

But mostly this book is the result of serendipity.

On 22 December 2024 the stars aligned and fate introduced me to Barrie Moreton, who gave me unprecedented access to the surviving Magic Bus company archives, including many previously unseen documents, letters and photographs, which Barrie had kept stored in his attic for over thirty-five years.

My advice to readers is simple.

Be lucky.

Richard Gregory
Shepherd's Bush

Table of Contents

The Background — 1
Magic Buses, Greg Williams, The Overland

The Original Bus — 8
The facts about the first Magic Bus to India

The Bus Company — 38
The first coaches and the early offices

The Travel Agent — 90
A new business model for the company

The Expansion — 116
Success and failure in Europe and beyond

The Implosion — 144
The company collapse and failed revival

The Aftermath — 158
What Greg Williams did next

The Legacy — 170
Memories, ephemera and sundries

The Mythology — 190
Misinformation and social media

The Epilogue — 212

66 Shaftesbury Avenue, London W.1.
01 439 8471 · Telex 21194

Chapter 1
THE BACKGROUND

Introduction

This story should have been told 40 years ago.

Once upon a time - in this case in the 1970s - the phrase 'Magic Bus to India' was heard across Europe in many languages, with the company name used for any cheap bus that did the journey, especially if it picked up passengers in Amsterdam.

The brand was notorious back then but almost nothing is known about the company itself. Tony Wheeler of *Lonely Planet* has even suggested that it didn't actually exist.

Those of us who lived in Europe at the time remember Magic Bus advertising in the press, and countless thousands of young people used the company - which, after a shaky start, became a booking agency rather than a bus operator in 1975.

So what follows is an attempt to tell the true story of Magic Bus, based on research and documentary evidence - because much of what I have seen written elsewhere is just fantasy.

Caveat

The author wasn't there. This account was pieced together using Magic Bus founder Greg Williams' personal archive, press cuttings, advertisements, and the memories of people involved.

Written sources are Graham Bourne's book *The Overlanders*, Carrie Cuneo's brief online testimony, posts on various web forums over the years and the contemporary media archives.

Testimony was also supplied by Cornelia Olsen, Barrie Moreton, Copenhagen Barry, Peter Stephenson, Alan Henderson, Torkild Bangsbo Andersen, Maarten Bolluijt, Rodda Thomas, Marisa, Nigel Howell, Graham Paton and anonymous contributors.

So the story begins.

The Magic Bus by Maurice Dolbier (1948).

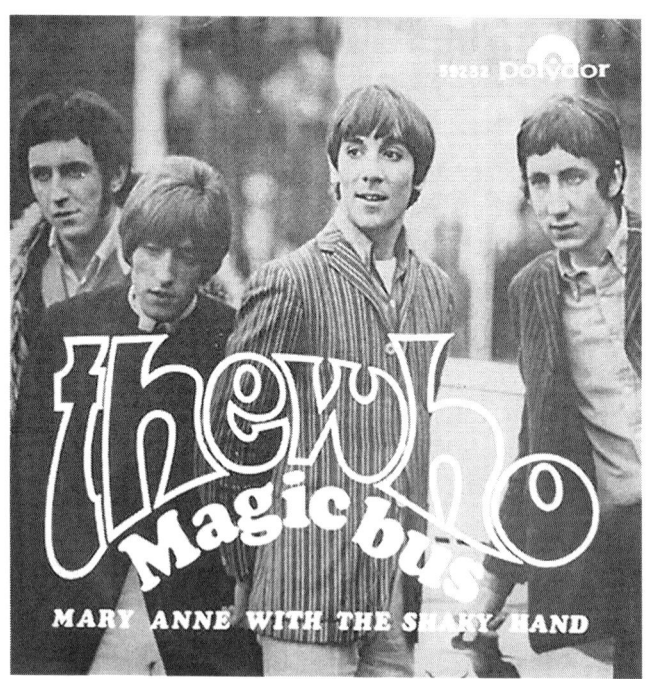

*Magic Bus by The Who (1968).
Note the Cooper Black font.*

Magic Buses

The earliest reference to a Magic Bus that I could discover was a children's book written by Maurice Dolbier and illustrated by Tibor Gergely, published in 1948 in USA and Canada.

The best-known Magic Bus is Pete Townshend's song, written for The Who in 1965 and released as a single in 1968, with the *Live At Leeds* version from 1970 a true classic. Most other uses derive from that song, including Townshend's short-lived bookshop.

The first actual bus known to have used the name was run by the Amsterdamse Mobiel Straet Circus Company de Magic Bus, doing tours of Amsterdam in the early 1970s. On 1 July 1972 a short piece appeared in the Dutch paper *NRC Handelsblad* under the headline *"Magic Bus is back"*, which recalled a *"beautifully painted vehicle"* that was a great success the previous year (a photograph exists). This time *"the Lowlands Weed Company"* would be involved, and the Magic Bus would leave twice a day from Museumplein *via* Rokin 24 - an address to remember.

Greg Williams was on friendly terms with the group, who advised the Amsterdam Chamber of Commerce on 1 July 1976 that he was *"authorised to register the name International Magic Bus under which title he is operating independently from de stichting de Amsterdamse Mobiel Straet Circus Company de Magic Bus since August 1, 1975"*.

There have been many other 'magic bus' projects since then - the name was popular with fundraising ventures in UK (one involved Jimmy Savile) and was later revived commercially by the Stagecoach company. On the other hand, Ken Kesey's bus 'Further' crossed the USA in 1964 but was not referred to as a 'magic bus' until 45 years later, it seems. Never trust a Prankster.

But this is the story of the Magic Bus company founded by Greg Williams, which started out as a small 'off the record' affair and became a household name for young people all over Europe.

Greg Williams

Gregory Clive Francis Williams was born on Monday 6 March 1950 at St Brenda's Nursing Home in Clifton, Bristol. His father was Frank Edward Reginald Williams, occupation dental surgeon, and his mother was Pauline Mary Williams (*née* O'Leary). Their home address is given on Greg's birth certificate as 132 Cranbrook Road, Redland, Bristol.

Greg had an elder brother named Nicholas, born two years earlier. At some point the family relocated to 36 Roslin Road South, Talbot Woods, Bournemouth, a detached house in a leafy suburb.

Greg presumably grew up there and went to school in the area, but as far as I am aware he never spoke about his early life.

Greg Williams' mother passed away in 1974. A copy of his paternal grandmother's will shows that he inherited a windfall while living in Amsterdam. Compared to some folks he was from a comfortable background, but not a wealthy one.

Copenhagen Barry

Greg Williams was in his late teens when he first met Copenhagen Barry, a Bournemouth native who was a year or so older. Greg was interested in the motor trade, and car ownership was expanding rapidly at the time. The sixties were swinging.

Barry recalled the local scene:

"On the one hand Bournemouth had long been a holiday resort", he told me, *"and a favourite place for retirement"* (which it still is - the area offers warm weather and good beaches by UK standards).

"On the other hand it was also a town with many language schools in the 1960s, attracting foreign students from France, Germany, Switzerland and Scandinavia".

As for the indigenous youngsters, Barry remembered a couple of local 'faces' named David and Bobby Singer, who traded in used cars from their home. One day they bought a second-hand Jaguar for £20 from a couple of teenagers who had turned up in their front yard with the engine running - only to discover later that the vehicle actually had no gearbox.

One of the terrible teenagers was Roger Coles, whose father was a local councillor. The other was Greg Williams.

Soon afterwards Greg shifted his operation to a basement flat in London near Earl's Court. It seems likely that 'business' was done in cash and that formalities were disregarded - it was a different world back then and I remember working 'off the cards' myself on occasion. God bless Hooky Street.

As Barry tells it, Greg and a few friends set off for India in two cars, one a Mercedes. It was the 1970s, the Hippie Trail was in full swing and many other young Europeans were doing the same kind of thing - believe it or not, it was actually *fashionable*.

But Greg was in fact being paid by a wealthy English woman to deliver the Mercedes (a white 300SE) to what was then still called Ceylon (now Sri Lanka) - and on the day before he got there the government had banned the import of foreign vehicles.

Later documents in Greg's archive suggest that he then bought some antique carvings in Tamil Nadu and either drove or had them shipped to Delhi, where he left them with a Mrs Dunkley.

Another document shows that on 27 May 1971 he bought an old Morris van in Delhi. He then drove it to Kabul with passengers on board before making his way back home by other means.

Barry told me that Greg, on his return to England, took on another Bournemouth 'face' named David Hurd as an assistant and went into the overland bus business.

The Overland

The history of overland travel from Europe to Asia begins with Alexander the Great, later encompassing the travels of Marco Polo and his family. But there are numerous other examples.

As for driving a vehicle to India, the honours go to Major FAC Forbes-Leith and his team, who took a Wolsey 15 from Leeds to Quetta in 1924 - and filmed the trip too. There were a few others between the wars, notably the Australian Francis Birtles.

In 1951 John Lennox Cook and Tim Hamilton-Fletcher rode a pair of Norton Dominators around the world from the UK, through Herat, Kandahar, Kabul, Lahore, Delhi and Agra to Colombo, then across Australia and across the USA.

In 1954 a mountaineering group from Cambridge led by George Brand drove a Bedford Dormobile to Rawalpindi, the first of many microbuses on the road, and in 1955 the Australian writer David McKay and his wife Betty drove a Volkswagen Kombi from Bombay to London *via* Kashmir, Afghanistan and Lebanon.

Tim Slessor, Eric Edis, Peter Townsend and Roy Follows later led four-wheeled expeditions to Singapore using the wartime Ledo Road through Burma, but it was not maintained and very quickly became impassable as the jungle reclaimed the land.

In 1958 the Women's Overland Himalayan Expedition to Zanskar featured three ladies driving a Land Rover from England as far as Manali, walking the rest of the way and returning *via* Afghanistan, camping in the desert. Their story is told in Antonia Deacock's book *No Purdah In Padam*.

There were many other pioneers, and not all of them wrote books about their exploits. The idea of a regular commercial bus service, however, was the brainchild of a former RAF man who had been in business selling vehicle parts in Asia.

The Indiaman

Paddy Garrow-Fisher was born in Ireland in 1914, served in Burma in World War II, and had already made trips between London and India by motorcycle and car before he started his bus company. His original idea had been to convert a coach into a mobile office and showroom, one that also provided sleeping quarters. He was on his first eastbound trip when the 1956 Suez crisis erupted - so he turned back to London to reconsider.

"I began to think of a tourist coach service to India. That seemed something I was fairly well qualified to do. I knew every route. I knew a few languages. I had friends in almost every town on the way, and I liked showing things to people. Above all, I knew it was possible to drive a bus right through to India provided it was the right sort of vehicle to start with... The more I pondered the idea the more I liked it".

The first Indiaman bus left London on 15 April 1957, reaching Calcutta on 5 June, and arrived back at Victoria Coach Station on 2 August. Paddy drove, with 18 passengers on board (some doing the return trip) along with his Indian wife Moti.

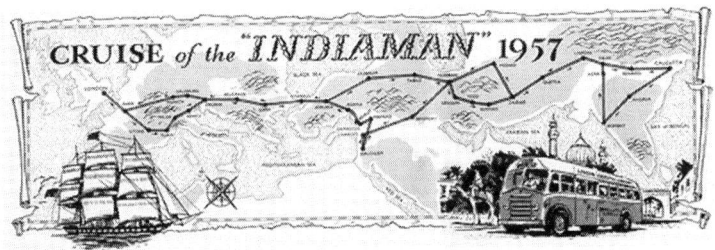

The Indiaman continued to run regular trips to India until 1971, when the brand name was sold to Penn Overland.

Paddy Garrow-Fisher passed away in 1975, by which time I had been on a bus to India myself - and the Magic Bus company was already on its way to becoming synonymous with the trip.

66 Shaftesbury Avenue, London W.1.
01 439 8471 · Telex 21194

Chapter 2
THE ORIGINAL BUS

Main Offices in: London·Amsterdam·Paris·Athens

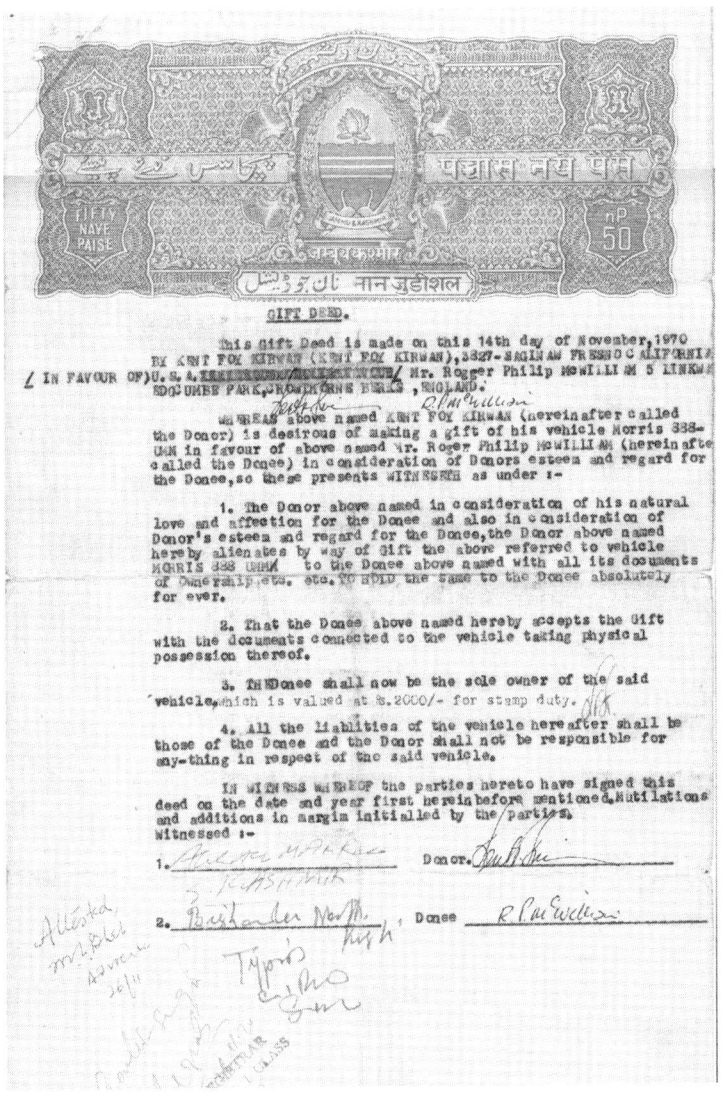

The vehicle that became the Magic Bus was imported to India on 20 September 1970 by Kent Foy Kirwan of California and signed over to Roger McWilliam on 14 November in Kashmir. Greg Williams acquired it on 26 May 1971 in Delhi.

The History Draft

There are few details known about Greg Williams' time in India. One document in the archive - undated, but featuring the classic logo and a Rokin 24 address in Amsterdam - offers a draft 'History' of the company on a single side of A4:

"The Original Magic Bus was purchased by the Originator in Delhi, India, in 1970", it begins, adding that *"it had to be driven immediately out of the country upon purchase"* for the paperwork to meet India's strict rules about foreign vehicles.

But other archive documents show that the bus only became the property of Greg Williams on 26 May 1971, having previously been acquired in Kashmir in November 1970 by a Roger McWilliam of Berkshire - and he had got it from a Kent Kirwan of Fresno, California. Both transactions were notarised as gifts, presumably to avoid any tax issues. God bless Hooky Street.

The hyperbolic 'History' continues:

"Therefore a trip to Kabul, Afghanistan was advertised at $10 a head, and surprisingly enough there were 30 enthusiastic riders in the space of a few hours. Two days later they were in Kabul, Afghanistan, black with dirt and exhausted, but they really had a good time. That was the first Magic Bus Trip".

I travelled the route myself in 1974. Delhi to Lahore would take a full day, Lahore to Peshawar a full day, and Peshawar to Kabul a full day. Colour me sceptical.

The bus had a top speed of 40 miles per hour and the journey took in two border crossings (both closed at night) plus the Khyber Pass and the Kabul Gorge. The entire route was along the Grand Trunk Road and there were no motorways. A quick web search offers a 'distance by road' of anything between 800 and 3,000 miles, while Google Maps simply admitted defeat and wouldn't give a distance at all. Your mileage may vary.

According to the 'History' draft:

"Soon thereafter, the little bus was transformed by mechanics, artists and body builders in Peshawar, Pakistan. They fitted it out complete with wrought-iron roof rack, gold lamé seats, paintings inside and out, 25 different coloured lights, and big painted banners on the sides saying 'Europe' and 'Asia' in English and in Urdu. This transformation took two and a half months but was well worth the wait".

"The Original Magic Bus was a sight to behold as it plyed through the desert at night, all lights dazzly and winking at the other vehicles on the road", the document claims.

Graham Bourne, in his memoir *The Overlanders*, quotes another version of the story that Greg told him in 1974:

"After they were finished paintin' it", he'd said, laughing at the memory, *"they fitted little coloured lights all over the place. They were 'anging along the length of the bus, around the windows, inside and outside. Made it look like a carnival float, they did! I wanted to drive back to England like that, but I 'ad to take 'em all down after a few miles 'cause they kept emptying the battery. The dynamo couldn't keep up the chargin' rate!"*

Bourne, who had found the bus neglected and decaying outside a Dutch barn some time in April 1974, also described it as *"an old, flat-nosed, twenty-seater Ford"* and *"a relic of the peace movement"* - wrong on both counts - so I wouldn't say that he is a particularly reliable source. But then neither was his employer, it seems.

Greg Williams' hyperbolic 'History' describes the original bus as *"truly Magical since it did the run from London to Delhi many times"*, with the word 'many' apparently doing some heavy lifting.

Documents in the archive attest that Greg Williams acquired the vehicle on 26 May 1971, and all sources agree that it was driven to Kabul soon afterwards - it seems likely that the Carnet de Passage had expired and was no longer valid.

Cornelia Gaines

I first heard of Cornelia 'Nee' Gaines in 2007, when her name was mentioned in a post on Derek Amey's *India Overland* forum by bus driver John Hackney:

"It was also around 1971/72 that I first met Greg and Nee of Magic Bus. At the time they were, I think, still running their own bus which was spectacularly painted in classic Pakistani designs (mountains, trees, lakes, birds etc). Soon afterwards they moved to Amsterdam and set up their booking office subcontracting fast Magic Bus trips to India".

Born in Charleston, West Virginia, Nee first met Greg Williams in November 1971 - she was living in London at the time and saw a card in a shop window in Notting Hill.

"Bus going to India", it said.

The Hippie Trail had been in full swing since 1967, with the number of 'freaks' hitting the road increasing year on year as the idea spread - there had even been a BBC documentary in 1970.

Inspired by the advertisement, Nee met with Greg Williams and his assistant David Hurd in Chiswick.

"They were both dressed in white boiler suits and the bus seemed inviting: it was a red and cream Bedford coach with 41 seats and oak leaves on the upholstery", she told me, a late 1950s model.

"We left on 11 December 1971", Nee recalled. The India-Pakistan war was underway at the time and the border remained closed to road traffic for several months.

"I never set foot in India (except at the Ferozepur bridge)", Nee told me in an email exchange, *"because the border was closed the entire time I was in Afghanistan and Pakistan".*

According to Nee, the original bus was *"a former Oxford University Press van, painted plainly orange and white... [Greg] intended to use it to transport stone sculptures"* (about which more later).

Nee confirmed that the bus was converted in Peshawar in early 1972 - she travelled back to London in it with Greg driving, was present when he got a new log book on 6 July, and was on board when they went to Cornwall to visit Copenhagen Barry.

After that she flew home to USA, while Greg took the bus on its final journey *via* Amsterdam to India and back, then flew to the States to join her for a family Xmas.

Cornelia 'Nee' Gaines. Photograph by Barrie Moreton.

Observant readers will notice that Nee's testimony is somewhat at odds with the various accounts of the Magic Bus origin story that Greg Williams gave during his lifetime.

That is because all the accounts Greg gave were fiction.

Mythmaking

"Greg Williams, a Briton, bought himself an old bus and recruited a load of like-minded passengers who also wanted to head east. But first he applied some paint and turned the bus into a spectacle that struck some observers dumb. One stayed calm enough to say, "That's magic!" and thus a great name was born".

So wrote Jane Morse in a *Washington Post* piece on 19 April 1981. The idea that Greg Williams *"applied some paint and turned the bus into a spectacle"* is nonsense - the vehicle was actually decorated by specialists who earned a living painting the trucks that ran between Pakistan and Afghanistan. The 1976 book *Afghan Trucks* by Jean-Charles Blanc offers many photographs of such vehicles but my understanding is that they were painted in Pakistan. As for the idea that a passenger was responsible for the brand name, it would more likely have been inspired by *Live At Leeds*, which was hugely popular at the time and ended with *Magic Bus*.

Graham Paton

Graham Paton had spent part of 1971 on a kibbutz in Israel and was heading for Goa that winter. Arriving in Kabul he found that the India-Pakistan war was underway and the border was closed.

"A story circulated about a 'magic bus' that could take us to Karachi", Graham told me. *"They had secured tickets on the first commercial flight from Karachi to Bombay"* (the road was still closed).

This was in January 1972, and the bus was the one that Nee had travelled on from London - they shared the trip to Lahore, unaware of each other. Graham remembered *"three young Dutch women"* and *"Elizabeth, an English journalist"* being on board.

"Luggage was stored on the roof", Graham added, including *"the worldly belongings of an English lady, daughter of the Raj, returning to her erstwhile home. She might have been sixty"*.

"To begin with I thought we were all stranded European and American travellers and it wasn't long before great clouds of hashish smoke were rolling down the aisle. Said English lady declined each chillum with a polite no thank you".

"The presence of more indigenous passengers became very vocal and obvious when we started negotiating the twists and turns of the Khyber Pass. A great wail of prayer and intercession would climax as we slung round each hairpin".

Graham remembered there being two drivers (who would be Greg Williams and David Hurd) and the bus radiator boiling dry, with an *ad hoc* system rigged up to keep it replenished from the cabin.

"Sleeping overnight outside under the moonlight at an inn with wooden-framed beds strung with canvas strapping... breakfasting on local tea and chapatis cooked at the roadside on an old primus".

"We arrived in Lahore to a city in foment and had to be chaperoned by police through a baying crowd to the hotel. I don't understand Urdu but they were not shouting words of welcome".

Greg and Nee returned to Kabul from Lahore, while David Hurd drove the bus to Karachi, arriving just in time for the passengers to catch the flight. He then drove it back to Europe, where it was written off in an accident in Austria - the top of the vehicle was removed by a low roof at a customs post, with nobody hurt.

Greg still had the white Mercedes that he had first used to drive to India, and the Morris van in Kabul, but without a Carnet they would have been confined to Afghanistan and Pakistan.

Greg had in fact acquired a Carnet for the Morris van in London in November 1971, and in early 1972 the vehicle was converted, fitted out and spectacularly painted in Peshawar.

Its next journey would be to England.

The Carnet

A 'Carnet de Passage en Douane' is a booklet containing many customs declaration forms (and counterfoils) used for temporary importation of a vehicle - it was required to transit countries such as Iran, exempting the driver from paying a substantial cash guarantee on entry (and the hassle of getting it back on exit).

A Carnet for the original bus was issued on 1 November 1971 by the AA in London, giving Greg's name and his family address in Bournemouth. But the bus itself was actually still in Asia.

Carnet issued by the AA in London on 1 November 1971.

The Carnet would have been needed to bring the bus back through Iran, the one country that insisted upon it for transit. It would have been carried on the Bedford bus that left London with Nee on board in December 1971.

The 'original' bus would now be free to travel again.

The Log Book

The registration states that the original bus was in fact a Morris 4 ton van, first registered on 25 March 1959, number plate 888 UMM with a diesel engine (1000cc on the Carnet).

The vehicle was registered to Greg Williams at 147 Sutton Court Mansions, Chiswick, London W4 - I happen to know that there is no number 147 in Sutton Court Mansions (on Grove Park Terrace) but there will be one in the mansion blocks at Sutton Court itself (on Sutton Court Road).

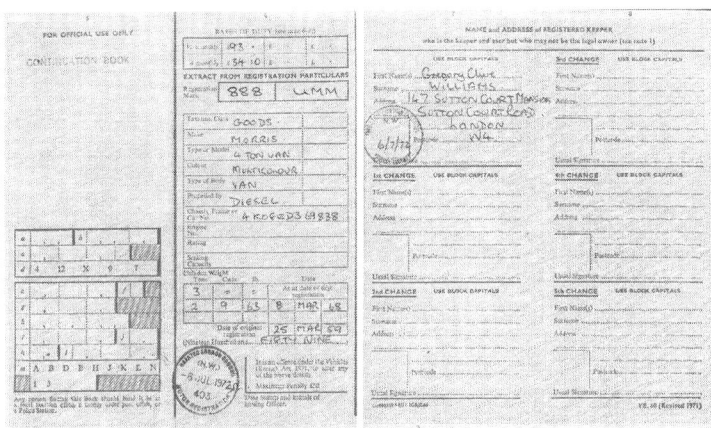

Log Book for the original Magic Bus issued by the Greater London Council on 6 July 1972.

Even the Brentford & Chiswick Local History Society has been known to make the same mistake. Whether Greg Williams ever actually lived there remains unclear.

Now back in England, Greg and Nee drove in the original painted Magic Bus from London down to Cornwall, about 250 miles, to visit Greg's old friend Copenhagen Barry.

It was a spectacular return.

*The only photograph of the Magic Bus in the archive.
The bus was cream, not white.*

*The original Magic Bus in Cornwall, July 1972.
Photograph courtesy of Copenhagen Barry.*

Peninsular West

As obscure publications go, *Peninsular West*, which only lasted a couple of years and served only Cornwall, may be one of the least known. But it does have a unique claim to fame.

"The Magic Bus That Came To Cornwall" was a puff piece written by a friendly journalist, complete with a splendid photograph of the vehicle, that appeared in a July 1972 issue:

"A young man who drove to India from London to get away from it all, built the bus from an old 1959 Morris diesel truck he had been using for carrying goods about in Delhi", said the article. *"He fitted it with windows and 24 gold cloth coloured seats, an ornate wrought iron roof-rack stretches along the length of the roof"*.

"The bus then went to Pakistan where an artist friend painted scenes of different countries, natives, lions, tigers and tropical birds inside and out. Around the top is a picture of a steam train with native drivers".

Greg Williams says that he had owned three buses *"but never quite got them all running at once due to having to rebuild the engines himself at each journey's end"*.

He then complains about the strict regulations in the 'Common Market' countries, which involve *"lots of terrible paperwork, much more hustle, headaches and expense"*.

"The 'Magic Bus' that came to Cornwall has made two trips", the piece continues. The fare to Delhi was said to be £35 and the journey took about 25 days.

"The bus will go from London to Delhi again as soon as there are 24 people to just 'chip in' with bread to beat the system", the article ends. *"This time the 'Magic Bus' does not return"*.

It didn't return to Cornwall, that's for sure.

Amsterdam

The Magic Bus next surfaced in Amsterdam on 9 August 1972, when the Dutch newspaper *Het Parool* printed a photograph of Greg Williams with the vehicle, on its first visit to the city, due to depart for Kathmandu the next day.

"There is room for 24 passengers and so far I have eighteen who are going", said Greg Williams, who was charging 320 guilders for the full trip to Nepal. The journalist was clearly impressed with the decoration of the bus: *"Apart from the paintings, depicting nature scenes but also steam locomotives, the benches are covered with a gold-coloured fabric and the interior, with its numerous knick-knacks and frills, looks a bit like an oriental tea garden".*

Magic Bus in Amsterdam, Het Parool 9 August 1972. Greg Williams is on the right of the photograph.

Greg Williams' age is given in the article as 23. According to his birth certificate he would in fact have celebrated his 22nd birthday on 6 March 1972, so something was amiss there - but at least they spelled his name correctly.

Tubantia

On the Saturday another obviously rehashed report - featuring *"Greg Williams, a 23-year-old Londoner"* - appeared in *Tubantia*, with another good photograph of the vehicle, and a week later the *Leeuwarder Courant* also offered a few words from *"Greg Williams, 23 years old and from London"* in a short piece.

Magic Bus in Amsterdam, Tubantia 12 August 1972.
The bus had left for Kathmandu two days earlier.

The Scoop

The real scoop, though, came in the *Algemeen Dagblad*, with Paul Lensink joining the bus for a week and posting two articles. They were in Dutch, so I ran them through an online translator. The first one, on Saturday 12 August, notes a familiar smell:

"The youngsters are making their long journey in search of - who knows. They don't say they know themselves. They call it adventure, the completely different culture, but especially the cheap hashish". Mkay.

The journalist actually gets Greg Williams' age right (22) - but calls him 'Grig' throughout (he rectified the error the next week). And we get another variation on the Magic Bus history:

"The condition of the bus is sometimes worrying. But driver and owner Grig Williams (22) from London says that he has already been to Nepal and back three times this year with this bus... After each trip the engine had to be overhauled".

The claim that Greg had *"been to Nepal and back three times this year with this bus"* is nonsense, but I wouldn't blame Paul Lensink for that - he probably just reported what he was told.

The land border between Pakistan and India was closed in December 1971 at the outbreak of the war over Bangladesh and it did not reopen to vehicle traffic for several months.

According to Nee, Greg had left London on 11 December 1971 driving the Bedford bus, which went to Lahore and Karachi. The 'original' bus could not enter India or Iran without a valid Carnet and I have seen no evidence that it ever reached Nepal. As we have seen, it was converted and painted in Peshawar in spring 1972, furnished with the new Carnet brought from London, and was back in England by 6 July 1972.

It is clear that Greg Williams gave several contradictory accounts of the Magic Bus origin story, and all of them were false.

Back on the bus in August 1972 our reporter noted a considerable intake of *hashish*. *"On every trip, this bus is full of drugs from top to bottom"* says Greg. *"Customs searches at every border. They have never been able to find anything".*

Paul Lensink's second report followed on 19 August, after he had flown home from Belgrade, and noted that the bus should have been in Istanbul by then. He passed on *"lots of love from Greg, Pat, Rita, Ross, Steve, Lee, Allen, Hanz, Andy, Peter, Sue, George, Bob, Mike, Mark, Blenda and all the others".*

"The exhaust is as leaky as a sieve, the engine is slurping oil, after exactly 386 kilometres the bus lost its front. A day later the starter broke down, so that the bus had to be pushed after every rest stop". Lost its front? I'm not sure that translated well.

"For a week I lived like an overaged hippie", the intrepid Lensink continues, adding that the passengers were *"boys and girls from America (more than half), England, Australia, Canada, Switzerland, Sweden and Austria".*

"At night we slept in our sleeping bags in the open air... there was always a traveling companion who made a 'joint' (a stick that everyone could take a puff of)... Most of the young passengers of the "Magic Bus" went to the Eastern countries in search of adventure and in search of the cheap drugs they could get there".

Bob Morgan from Ohio, Françoise Dutour and Laurent Michel (both from Paris) and an Australian named Ross King all get a full name-check, as does Steve McGlinchey, aged 18.

The journalist praises the spirit of the group, who all seem to be getting along very well with each other, but can't help remarking that *"the only thing that occasionally spoils the atmosphere is the sweet smell of hash".* Mkay.

There are several photographs in the two articles showing the bus and passengers, but I only have low quality versions (some from an old photocopy amongst Greg Williams' papers). Good prints may still lurk in an archive somewhere in Holland.

Magic Bus was clearly something of a novelty in Amsterdam - there were several pieces on the departure in the Dutch newspapers, and no suggestion that there was ever an earlier service using the same name on the route to India in the 1960s.

But while the Dutch press was very clear that the bus was bound for Kathmandu in 1972, I have seen no evidence that it actually got there - and Greg himself always spoke of trips to Delhi.

The Dunkley Dispute

Amongst the surviving papers in Greg Williams' archive is a letter from a Mrs P Dunkley, who gives an address in Parliament Street, New Delhi, that is dated 9 October 1972.

It is a complaint to a *"Mr Vijay Dhar, C/o Dr Shivji Dhar, Behind State Hospital, Nawa Bazar, Sri Nagar, Kashmir"*, and it concerns some items that the writer claims have not been returned.

"As you know, certain wood-carvings that you took away from my home belonged to a Mr Greg Williams who purchased them and holds receipts for them. Now Mr Williams has returned to collect them. Kindly return them to me so I can give them to him".

This effectively confirms that the Magic Bus from Amsterdam that left in August had reached Delhi, at least.

Mrs Dunkley, who says she has been unwell and has had financial worries, is concerned to get her belongings back:

"You know very well that Maureen was very fond of you and I regarded you as a son and was also quite fond of you and still I have confidence that you will return my things intact".

A list of items is attached - it includes some watches and clocks, a typewriter, a tape recorder, a tape of Bob Dylan's *Nashville Skyline*, some jewellery, an antique book in Urdu, 1500 rupees in cash, Greg Williams' wood carvings *"including 2 stone slabs, carved; carved stone head; several stone statuettes, etc"* valued at 10,000 rupees, and *"some other items"*.

The receipt mentioned is from the Murugan Arts Emporium of Kayangundu Lane, Kallukatti, Tamil Nadu. It has no date on it.

The archive does not record whether Greg or Mrs Dunkley ever got their belongings back, but it seems unlikely.

```
LIST OF ARTICLES TAKEN ON TRUST
BY MR. VIJAY DHAR.
                                                              Value
 1.  Hitachi Tape-Recorder, Stereophonic          Rs.  2,000
 2.  National    "         "                                   300
 3.  Orient Watch, Japanese (automatic, time, date,
     compass, etc.)                                           1,000
 4.  Omega Watch (Black dial)                                  400
 5.  Travelling clock, colour red.                              60
 6.     "         "        "   black, brand new                150
 7.  Sleeping Bag, pink, nylon wool, new                     1,000
 8.  Olivetti semi-portable typewriter                       1,000
 9.  Cigaretter lighter marked "V.I.P."                        200
10.  Burglar Alarm                                             100
11.  Tape (Bob Dylan - Nashville Skyline)                       20
12.  2 Night suits, brand new                                   80
13.  1 large Burma Ruby         current value not known-
                                to be valued.
14.  1 small Ruby                       -do-
15.  1 Amber necklace (40 or 50 beads approx.) -do-
16.  Air mattress                                               30
17.  Gold Ring - with stones                                   500
18.  1 antique book in Urdu     To be valued. High value.
19.  Wood Carvings (including 2 stone slabs, carved;   10,000
                   carved stone head; several stone statuettes, etc.)
20.  Some other items.
21.  Rs.1500/- in cash.
```

P. Dunkley (Mrs.)

*Mrs Dunkley's list of missing items.
Note item 19, which includes carved stone slabs,
a carved stone head and several stone statuettes,
all the property of Greg Williams.*

Carl Saffioti

The *'IndiaMike'* online forum, 24 April 2020:

"I met Greg Williams of Greg and Nee fame in Delhi in 1972. At that time the vehicle which was called Magic Bus was I think a possibly Bedford van with windows cut in the side and painted like a Pakistan/Indian truck. I travelled with Greg and a few others from Delhi to Kabul and on to Amsterdam. We slept in the bus in a field just out of Amsterdam. Nobody had any money and it was extremely cold".

The testimony is from Carl Saffioti. Like a few other characters in this tale he is mostly known from a couple of posts on minor web forums, but his testimony does seem credible and it reveals some details about a little-known period of Magic Bus history.

There is no confirmation that the bus reached Kathmandu, but it did make it back to Amsterdam from Delhi. As we shall see, it went no further than Gelderland after that.

Nee described Carl Saffioti as *"a loyal booking agent for Magic Bus in Amsterdam, standing patiently in front of American Express, wearing a sandwich board and taking deposits on trips to Athens, Istanbul and India. He did this before we had an office in the city, and probably after as well"*.

Carl says that he accompanied Greg Williams to London in 1973 (purpose unknown) and that his hustling on Damrak earned him a free ride to Nepal as winter approached.

On that occasion he travelled on a bus driven by Neil Stevens and Graham Styles, with Neil's girlfriend Barbara also on board.

Carl wasn't on the return trip but a Canadian named Keith Rajala was, and kept a diary. It seems that the bus only made it as far as the Caspian Sea in Iran, but Keith continued to travel overland to England with Graham Styles, arriving in mid-January 1974.

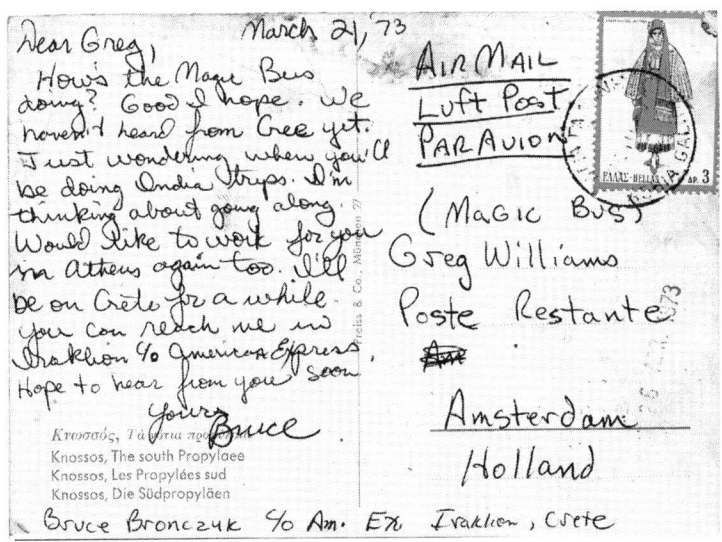

Bruce Bronczyk

The only document in Greg Williams' archive known to be from 1973 is a postcard, dated 21 March, from a Bruce Bronczyk in Crete - addressed to Greg at *"Poste Restante, Amsterdam"*.

"Dear Greg, How's the Magic Bus doing?", the postcard begins, *"Good I hope"*. Bruce expresses an interest in joining a future India trip, which suggests at least some knowledge of Greg's activities. *"Would like to work for you in Athens again too"*, he adds.

This was just three months after the original bus had returned to Holland for the last time. With no advertising and no offices the Magic Bus company was still very much under the radar.

Copenhagen Barry recalled that Greg had bought a few used buses in 1973 and begun operating on the Amsterdam to Athens run, ignoring any regulations. It seems likely that Magic Bus was not formally registered as a company anywhere at this point, and even more likely that it paid no taxes.

Zeeland

Nee told me she had joined Greg in Holland in February 1973, renting a house near Wemeldinge, a village in Zeeland, along with driver Neil Stevens. Nee remembered it as windy, wet and foggy, but the villagers were friendly and quaintly old-fashioned:

"There were still some traditional Dutch costumes around. Many people wore wooden shoes, and the ladies wore long billowy dresses with bonnets and strange gold flaps on either side of their head, like blinders on a horse's bridle, only sticking out horizontally".

Greg had bought three used AEC buses from a local company that had a workshop there, each one named after a European mountain: Col d'Izoord, Monte Gioveretto and Zugspitze.

"We had gotten one of them in excellent running order and it was in first class condition", Nee recalled. *"A 50-seater coach complete with icebox and other luxurious touches, with lots of varnished wood inside. We drove it up to Amsterdam (a three hour drive) and back again, and it seemed very good".*

At some point Greg had been introduced to Ab Van Asch, who had a business repairing and selling cars - something that Greg could clearly relate to - and lived with his wife Ricky and their young sons Mario and Freddy near Beesd in rural Gelderland.

The property was in a village called Rumpt and included a field and a thatched barn, where a mechanic named Fritz (who lived nearby with his wife Hanneke) did repairs and maintenance.

The original painted Magic Bus had made it back to Amsterdam in the winter of 1972 but was no longer roadworthy, so Greg and Nee hooked it up to the AEC bus and towed it down to Rumpt. Nee recalled that *"the towbar snapped in the middle of Amsterdam in the pouring rain"*, but they got there eventually and parked the vehicle in the field behind the barn.

Rumpt

"Greg and I lived in the original Magic Bus in the field during that spring and summer. Baby goats lived underneath. We took out all the seats and had a big space there. I cooked over a gas bottle with a platform for pots and pans. We could use the shower and toilet in the house by the big ancient barn, and I washed the dishes in that sink too".

Nee learned basic Dutch from Mario and Freddy (who included basic obscenities) and had coffee and cake with the family and their friends every Sunday. She met Miss Van Asselberg, a retired doctor, who wore one red shoe and one green one and lived in an ancient thatched house, with chickens sitting on her knee as she bemoaned the effects of fluoride in the water supply. Country life was at times idyllic, but at other times confining.

Fritz and Hanneke told Greg and Nee about a large house for rent in Beesd, and they eventually took it on. It felt too big at first, but that soon changed as drivers came to stay.

"Carl Saffioti was booking passengers in front of American Express in Amsterdam", Nee told me. *"We would drive one of the AEC buses up to Amsterdam and pick the passengers up for a trip to Athens. Neil Stevens drove one of the others, and it was a great day when our two buses passed each other in Yugoslavia, one going north and one going south, stopped, backed up, and all the passengers got out and shook hands!"*

This was how the Magic Bus company got underway, though it was still unofficial and had no office. As Xmas approached Nee once again headed back to her family in USA.

"Greg had descended into a depression, and sat on the bed staring at the wall in a dark room. As much as he was a charismatic, dynamic person with huge ambition, drive, and charm, he crashed hard and could not find a way out of it".

Greg Williams had his demons.

Known Photographs

The only photograph of the original bus in Greg Williams' archive is an oversized negative, which was later supplied to the makers of *Some Liked It Hot* for their coffee table book, where it was mislabelled and only partially printed.

The 1972 photograph printed in *Peninsular West* was provided by Copenhagen Barry in 2024 and is very good quality, but all the others that I have seen are of a lesser standard.

There are shots of the bus and passengers in the Dutch press from August 1972 - *Het Parool, Tubantia* and *Algemeen Dagblad* all printed photographs. The copies I have are low quality, but there may still be better prints stored in the press archives.

Martin Duce posted on the web in December 2024 that he was aboard the bus from Istanbul to Delhi in 1971 - with a photograph from the Turkish press showing the bus, himself, Greg Williams and many other passengers. But he got the year wrong, as the bus was not converted and painted until spring 1972.

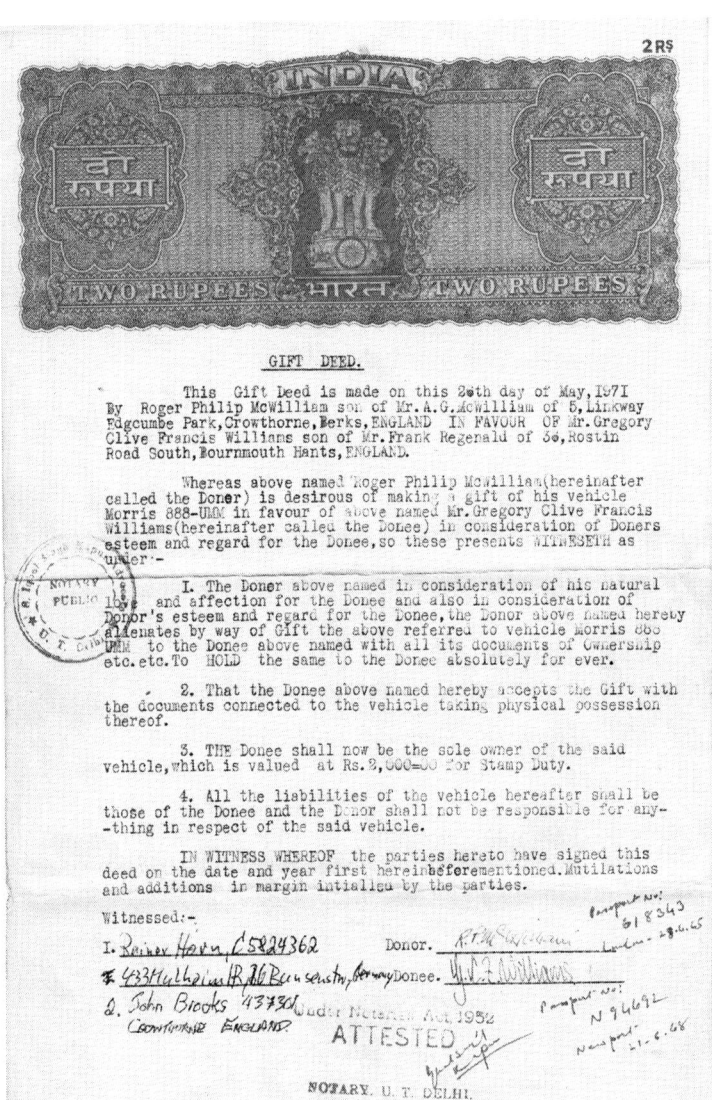

Greg Williams acquired the bus in Delhi on 26 May 1971. He gave many different versions of the Magic Bus origin story during his lifetime, all of them fictional.

The Bourne Legacy

For more than 25 years Graham Bourne's book was the primary source of information about the original Magic Bus - and almost everything he wrote about it was inaccurate.

When he first saw the vehicle decaying outside a barn in Rumpt in April 1974 he described it as *"an old, flat-nosed, twenty-seater Ford"* (it was a Morris with 24 passenger seats) and *"a relic of the peace movement"* (in fact it had previously been a delivery van for the Oxford University Press before it was driven to India).

"This was the bus Greg had used to drive a handful of hippies from London out to New Delhi several years earlier", Bourne writes, though it had left England less than two years before. He adds that Greg *"told me sometime later about the first return trip from Delhi, where he'd had the bus painted"* (it was painted in Peshawar).

In summer 1974 Bourne helped to dump the bus, which was by now deteriorating rapidly. He describes it as a *"rusty piece of Indian art"* that featured *"delicately encased scenarios of sunsets and snowy mountain ranges, elephant trains and Buddhas"*.

There were certainly trains, but no elephants and definitely no Buddhas. Why I am so confident? The answer lies in an eyewitness account from 1972 and the testimony of its author in 2025.

The Eyewitness Account

Part of a letter that Nee sent home from Peshawar in 1972:

"Greg goes down to the workshop every day to try to speed things up - like a regular job - but the old man who is doing the work calls him Sahib and makes him drink tea all day. They have a different attitude to work than we do".

"The work has been terribly slow - over two months instead of the proposed 10 days - but if you go to the workshop you can see why: it is a huge mud yard that takes a map to navigate almost, around the giant puddles and pools of solid, black oil".

"The old man uses only small boys to do the work (his own son, aged 12, is in there doing the work of a grown man) and employs a man only when absolutely necessary. All the work is done almost entirely by hand with the most simple tools, it is fascinating to watch. There is no electricity. At night they work by candlelight, and if it rains they don't come to work".

"The bus has gold lame seats (benches across, with the center seat backs folding forward and strong enough to walk on, so there is a central aisle). It has a wrought iron roof rack with a filigree ladder up the back of the vehicle. Inside and out it is covered with paintings: miles of super highways with Swiss chalets and mountains, boats floating in mirrored lakes, a lion attacking a panther, peacocks, garlands of flowers everywhere, an old-fashioned choo-choo on each side with Greg driving one and me driving the other, and two big ribbons that say "Magic Bus - Europe - Asia", in English and in Urdu, one on each side, and two little ribbons that say "Home-Sweet-Home" on the doors, and a big eagle on the front carrying a mysterious letter".

"Inside there are many fabric dingly-danglies, and camel decorations and woven curtains of many colors with little bells bordering them, a very dreamy sound. The ceiling inside is patterned black on cream, using sooty candles in circular motion to create the design, and then varnishing over to preserve it".

Afghan Trucks

Nee's contemporary eyewitness description from 1972 debunks the article by Jane Morse in the *Washington Post* from 1981 - which has Greg Williams painting the bus himself - as well as Graham Bourne's claim that the decoration was done in Delhi.

Peshawar, once the Afghan summer capital, is a city in north-west Pakistan, and the gateway to the Khyber Pass. It is a one-day journey by road through the border to Kabul.

Before I set out upon the Hippie Trail myself in 1974 a friend told me about the elaborately decorated commercial vehicles that were used on the Grand Trunk Road, which she and everybody else referred to as *"Afghan Trucks"*.

There was even a book with that title published in 1976, with a set of photographs taken by Jean-Charles Blanc, whose introductory text begins with a flight of fancy:

"Traditionally it was the custom of Afghan caravan-drivers to adorn their camels with bunches of ribbon, tassels, fringes and an array of good-luck charms, before embarking on their hazardous desert pilgrimages. They intended by the liberal use of these decorative symbols both to pay homage to their camels as custodians of their journey and to place them under the protection of God. For the spirits that haunted the wilderness were reputed to be evil".

"Today this tradition has survived in the form of paintings and flowers which festoon the sides of the Afghan truck".

But the trucks were not made in Afghanistan and were not painted there either - the tradition began in the early 20th century under the British Raj, when imported trucks were decorated by the locals (particularly in Punjab).

What we called 'Afghan Trucks' were generally Pakistani.

Afghan Trucks by Jean-Charles Blanc, 1976

A painted truck in Herat, Afghanistan, 1974.
Photograph by Richard Gregory

Magic Bus Requiem

Graham Bourne's *The Overlanders* contains a detailed account of the original Magic Bus being scrapped - though 'dumped' would be a more accurate description - on a country road just outside Rumpt sometime in summer 1974.

The book is no longer available for sale, so this is my transcription from a copy that is held by the British Library:

"I helped Fritz remove the chicken nests from their upholstered home in the back of the old bus, and together we loaded it with Greg's collection of parts. I was to have the honour of driving the wreck on its last journey, so Fritz gave me a blanket to drape over the filthy seat, and while he attached a long cable from his tow-truck to the front bumper, I used a wire brush to clean the encrusted droppings off the steering wheel. The interior was hot from the sun shining down on the metal roof and the smell was indescribable as I sat there among the feathers, but then the cable tautened, and with a jerk Fritz dragged us out of the bright sunlight into the dark barn. The creepers unravelled noisily from the outside mirrors as I was drawn through the workshop and up the drive onto the road, and my skin crawled as the rotten velvet tassels and spider's webs swung about me".

"The bus had stood neglected for so many years that the tyres hardly had any air left in them, and the sound of flopping rubber and flaking wheel rims was maddening, while steering it was nigh on impossible. Fritz towed me and the mystic painted jalopy along a seldom used lane for about two miles, while I fought to keep the thing in a straight line and not fly off at a tangent, until we finally reached a piece of wasteland in the middle of the countryside. Fritz stopped and walked back to unhook the cable, then laughed as he looked at me through the crap covered windscreen".

"You want to drive dis to Istanbul next time?"

I climbed out, and my wrists hurt from the shuddering.

"We can't leave it here", I said, looking around at the hedgerows and high corn. A bird swooped and landed on the bus's roof, bending its head to look at the elephants.

"Why not? Ze council come along and tow it away", then he laughed again, callously this time. "I bet they wonder where zat came from!"

The thought of some ordinary council workers scratching their heads over that rusty piece of Indian art made me laugh too, but it seemed a shame to just dump it after such an inglorious past. On the way back to the barn I said it belonged in a museum, but Fritz just spat out the window.

"Junk", he said, "nozing but junk!"

Well, that's what happened to the original Magic Bus. An ignoble end for a bus that had blazed the Hippy Trail, and baffled many an ignorant European with its portrayal of Indian art and culture. As I said, it really belonged in a museum".

It was not to be.

Algemeen Dagblad, 12 August 1972

66 Shaftesbury Avenue, London W.1.
01 439 8471 · Telex 21194

Chapter 3
THE BUS COMPANY

Main Offices in: London·Amsterdam·Paris·Athens

Graham Bourne's memoir The Overlanders was published in 1998 by Minerva, but the company folded soon after and the book is no longer available.

The second and third volumes were self-published and I have been unable to obtain copies.

*Original Magic Bus promotional material c1974,
probably used by the hustlers on Damrak.
Note the Rokin 24 address and phone number.*

The Damrak Hustle

The counterculture in Amsterdam was (and remains) different to that of other European capitals, and I'm not talking about putting mayonnaise on fries.

Dutch youth were not necessarily more radical than elsewhere, but they were much more successful when compared to London, where the 'legalise pot' movement achieved nothing, despite the support of luminaries such as The Beatles.

Activism in Amsterdam included an occupation of Dam Square, and while that was eventually cleared the main Dutch cities had a markedly more liberal attitude than neighbouring countries.

Before the Magic Bus company ever had an office Greg Williams used street hustlers armed with cardboard signs to drum up business, with the regular pitch on Damrak outside the American Express.

Why the American Express building? Because Americans had more money to spend than anyone else, it was as simple as that.

The First Flyer

What appears to be the oldest promotional material in the archive is a decidedly amateur A4 sheet, single-sided, probably produced on an early photocopier - it seems likely that it would have been used by the Damrak hustlers in summer 1974.

It gives the Rokin 24 address and a phone number, offering rides to Athens or Istanbul for $35 and Munich for $15. There is also a poorly reproduced photograph of some men in turbans sitting on the roof of a bus. Everything else is either handwritten or drawn, there is no typing at all.

But it was cheap and informative.

The Flyer Draft

Stapled to the flyers in the archive were a couple of handwritten sheets giving another draft origin story. This one has sections crossed out, and some parts that survive in other versions.

"Five years ago whilst bumming around the East with the proverbial pack on back and faded Levi's Greg Williams came across a battered old bus. It had been used for all manner of things by a hundred diffirent [sic] owners including Oxford University... Although we no longer run the original 'Magic Bus' we still keep it as a kind of good luck charm and we look after it like good children round a mother".

The Original Magic Bus Draft

This typed draft is clearly based on the 'Flyer Draft':

"Five years ago Greg Williams (founder of the Magic Bus Co.) whilst bumming about India with his pack on his back came across a battered old bus. It had been used for a variety of things by various different owners including Oxford University. Carrying everything from intense intellectums to sheep and chickens on its travels".

The piece states that Greg drove the bus to Afghanistan, where it was *"attacked by mechanics, body builders and artists (all friends)"* with the end result being a *"multicoloured picturesque tough reliable mode of transport"*. Don't believe the hype.

There's plenty of it:

"For three years he ran it to and from Delhi... suffering no serious breakdowns... hundreds of people from all over the world rode on the Magic Bus from Europe to India. Now some of those travellors [sic] who know the routes so well form the hardcore of the Magic Bus Company. The folk who kept in touch now help run this unique service with Greg. They all know most of the hassles and official problems of travelling with a limited amount of money".

"Although the original Magic Bus is no longer used of [sic] these expeditions it forms the nucleus of our depot in Holland", we are told. *"Like a mother it sits in the yard surrounded by its successors when they come in for servicing and is used as a store for the spare parts and doubles as an office"*.

The typed words *"and doubles as an office"* were later crossed out in pen. Graham Bourne's book describes the bus *"in a sorry state"* in a field near Beesd with chickens in residence in early 1974, before Magic Bus actually had an office.

So that's three undated documents telling different versions of the Magic Bus origin story, plus the 1972 accounts in *Peninsular West* and *Algemeen Dagblad*. All are fiction.

The Overland Adventure Draft

There is one more undated document in Greg Williams' archive that mentions the original bus, a two-page hand-written draft about the *'Overland Adventure'*, outlining the route, itinerary, cost and other details, probably dating from 1974:

"The fare of £35 from Amsterdam/Oostende to Delhi includes transport and the use of camping equipment only", we are told early in the piece. *"Magic Bus journies [sic] are designed for people who can't afford to travel in their own vehicle, but who would like to travel cheaply and more independently than is possible on a fancy, carefully planned tour"*.

"The journey is very flexible.. It takes from 3 to 6 weeks from Amsterdam/Oostende to Delhi... The coaches have 41 seats (except for the original and famous Magic Bus, which has 24) and plenty of space for 50 lbs of luggage per passenger".

The piece ends with the slogan *"Magic Bus Means Good Vibes"*. It does seem to suggest that the original bus was still seen as a going concern - but in fact its days were numbered.

Graham Bourne

Graham Bourne's 1998 book *The Overlanders* only covers about nine months of 1974 and offers little about the earlier history of the Magic Bus company. I couldn't find a copy for sale anywhere and could only read it at the British Library.

Fortunately I am blessed with a photographic memory (it came with the phone). Bourne was introduced to Magic Bus by Copenhagen Barry, who he knew from London, and who accompanied him to Greg Williams' headquarters in Beesd, Holland, to get him started in his new life on the road. It was March 1974.

"I learnt how to travel light", Bourne writes in his foreword, *"dodge border patrols, lie convincingly, look sober in front of policemen, and roll party-joints long enough to be shot from a bow"*.

Readers need to be aware that Bourne changes the names of some of the participants to avoid incriminating them in less than legal activities. He is sometimes factually inaccurate by mistake too, but none of us are immune to that.

Beesd

Graham Bourne arrived in Holland thinking he was going to be working as a tour guide, and was surprised to find himself assigned as second driver on a trip to Greece - whatever his other talents, he had never actually driven a bus before.

He soon got the hang of it, shuttling between Amsterdam and Athens (and later Istanbul), staying at Greg Williams' house in Beesd with other drivers between tours, even after switching to an independent bus owned by someone else.

Bourne confirms that Magic Bus deployed various hustlers with cardboard signs outside the American Express on Damrak, and tells of a financial scare in summer 1974 with rumours that the company was going out of business.

He also revealed that Greg Williams had personally 'upgraded' his standard driving licence to one suitable for an international bus driver - or at least looked like it.

"The service itself was only vaguely illegal", Bourne says in his book, *"but the disregard for the law during that time knew no bounds... The conniving and double-dealing was similar to that among pirates... There were no Eurocops with computer link-ups, nor were there any international agreements regulating public transport..."*

As Graham Bourne's book tells it, the Magic Bus company was all about *"illegally conveying young people back and forth in clapped-out old buses between the main capitals of Europe"*.

Bourne does mention the Asia trips but never left Europe himself and sheds no light on the 'Magic Bus to India', just a series of runs from Amsterdam to Athens and Istanbul.

He seems to have had plenty of fun on his travels. If a film had been made of his book it would probably have starred Robin Askwith and been called *"Confessions of a Magic Bus Driver"*.

Rokin 24

The only commercial office mentioned in Graham Bourne's book was opened at Rokin 24 in Amsterdam in July 1974 - it was a room manned by a guy named Canadian Bruce (who may or may not have been Bruce Bronczyk, who'd sent a postcard to Greg the previous year). Bourne describes his first visit:

"Soon I reached the Dam, and shortly after that I was looking for the house number on Rokin (the name of the street) where the Magic Bus office was to be found. From the number of posters plastered along the walls around one of the doors, it was obvious where to walk in, and, with increasing expectancy, probably due to the faint sweet smell that hung in the air, I climbed the narrow wooden staircase in a steep spiral to the fourth floor".

"The office was simply furnished", Bourne continues, *"with a desk on bare boards facing the door, some cluttered shelves, and in the corner on my left a couple of red seats from Tony's and Cathy's bus. Judging by the dense smoke, I'd found the source of the sweet smell and, sitting on a chair behind the desk, to all appearance incapable of sudden movement, was Bruce. He was one of Greg's hustlers I'd met on the pavement in front of the American Express, and his deep-set eyes stared at me through a pair of small, wire-rimmed glasses, as if unsure how long I'd been there".*

Bruce offered Bourne a joint, which they shared, then opened a window. Next he introduced Bourne to a pair of pink-eyed white mice, in a cage on the floor, which were as stoned as they were and (according to Bourne) *"lay stunned on their backs".*

Cockroaches were not mentioned.

Bruce later told Bourne over a beer that Greg Williams had moved out of the house in Beesd and that Copenhagen Barry, with his wife and child, had taken it over. Bourne doesn't say where Greg was now living, but a flat in Amsterdam seems likely.

Nieuwendijk

At some point Greg and Nee took on an apartment in the centre of Amsterdam above the shops at 57-59 Nieuwendijk.

Graham Bourne doesn't mention it in his book, but writes that in May that year, when the company was rumoured to be going bust, Kevin Buckley in Athens *"had tried to call Beesd and the office in Amsterdam but couldn't reach anybody"*.

I would guess that by 'the office' he may have meant Nieuwendijk, as his account of his visit to the room at Rokin 24 two months later explicitly describes it as the first public Magic Bus office, one that Greg Williams had only just opened.

But Graham Bourne's book does contain numerous inaccuracies, and he was far from central to the Magic Bus operation.

Magic Bus London

A trawl of the *Time Out* archives suggests that the first Magic Bus advertisement to appear in England was on 15 March 1974, giving no address but a phone number in Richmond:

"MAGIC BUS. Overland tours to Athens and India via Istanbul from 25. Phone for brochure and info etc. 01-940 3162".

The term 'brochure' may have been a slight exaggeration. Graham Bourne says in his book that in early May, just after visiting Jochen Reier, he had a conversation with Greg Williams in Beesd:

"I've been in London the last couple of weeks, tryin' to sort the office out", he quotes Greg as telling him. "*Got to go back there in a couple of days"*. But he gives no further details.

The 'office' was actually Copenhagen Barry's flat - he had agreed to help out for three months until he moved to Holland.

All Change

The last advertisement in *Time Out* from Magic Bus in Richmond appeared on 31 May, and the next one that my research could find was published in the *International Times* of 1 July 1974:

"MAGIC BUS overland to Athens, Istanbul £25.00p leaving every Saturday. Phone 01-263 0662 for details - right on!"

The telephone was installed at 27 Giesbach Road N19, a residential property close to Archway, and on 19 July the *Time Out* advertising resumed using the same number (but a different day):

"MAGIC BUS. Overland to Athens, Istanbul. £25. Leaving every Friday. 01-263 0662 for info".

At this point there was still just a single small ad for Magic Bus in *Time Out* each week, fairly insignificant amongst the competition - Budget Bus, Tangerine Travels, Exodus, Trail Finders, TenTrek and countless others were also listed.

Interspersed in the classified travel section there were also ads for BIT's *Overland to India and Beyond* (including information about *"dope"*), the *Truckers Bible* (a guide for cannabis smugglers from Release), and *Bust* (a topical board game about *hashish* smuggling and dealing). Those were the days...

Magic Bus then adopted a 'scattergun' approach with numerous small ads in *Time Out* for various destinations, and on 27 September the first box ad appeared, with an address (Giesbach Road) given for the first time on 15 November.

Floyd Webb worked for Magic Bus during *"the winter and spring of 1974-75"* as it moved to its first real office at 637 Holloway Road by 31 January 1975, when the box ad offered buses to Kabul for £50 and Delhi for £55. The company was on its way to dominating the market in the UK, which had a population over four times that of Holland. Things were looking up.

Connecticut

Meanwhile in Connecticut USA, the *Bridgeport Sunday Post* of 30 June 1974 had published a short article on page 30 with the title *'Branch Library To Open Exhibit Of Tibetan Art'*.

The exhibition, which ran for a full month at the Fairfield Woods branch library, featured *"Tibetan wood block prints and paintings"* and had been organised by *"David Gordon of Westport and Cornelia Gaines of Darien, who have traveled extensively in Eastern countries collecting the works of art"*.

BRIDGEPORT SUNDAY POST

The piece helpfully explains that *"Tankas are watercolor paintings on cloth, usually bordered by rich brocades and rolled like scrolls when not in use. In Tibet and other Buddhist countries they are considered religious rather than artistic objects, and are used primarily for the purpose of teaching the stories and principles of Buddhism, and for purposes of meditation"*.

"These paintings are completely alien to the Western eye", we are told, *"yet they glow with a serenity and mystical quality which will delight the viewer"*. As for the prints, the article says that they are *"made with a carved wooden block and are printed with black ink on paper made from the bark of a tree and yak-hide glue. They have been framed by Miss Gaines"*.

Nee and David apparently had useful input from Wesley Needham of the nearby Yale university. *"Each piece in the show is identified and described, so that the viewer will have some idea of the significance of the paintings and prints in their native land"*.

Nee later explained to me that she flew between USA and Europe fairly regularly - she worked hard at the Magic Bus office so would have needed a break now and then, and her family and friends were based in America.

Driving A Desk

It was Greg Williams himself who coined a rather cheeky term for what Nee did for the Magic Bus company - she *"drove a desk"* in Amsterdam and London, he said.

Nee was a founding partner of the business - and I've been told that she was actually *"the driving force"* of the Magic Bus company. Well, *someone* had to drive the desk, didn't they?

Greg and Nee took on the Nieuwendijk flat in 1974, moving from Beesd to Amsterdam and setting up their first Magic Bus office at Rokin 24 - in the same building as the Amsterdamse Mobiel Straet Circus Company de Magic Bus, which had run countercultural tours of the city since 1971.

"Departures were from Museumplein", said Nee, *"where Bernardus 'Pi' Pilippes' local Magic Bus left for its city tours, taking tourists to visit windmills and houseboats that served free grass tea. Pi would wear a top hat and roll out a red carpet at the designated parking place, which had an official 'Magic Bus' sign".*

"Robert Ragir was an American who lived on a houseboat and he sat at the desk all day and booked passengers. He taught me a lot of Dutch too! He introduced us to Bernard Stolte, a Dutchman who also sat at the desk all day, and gradually we began to develop a regular service to Athens".

"We kept under the radar of the authorities for a long time because of the legitimacy of that parking place and the assistance of the local Magic Bus company".

The local company does indeed seem to have been helpful, and Pi even wrote to the Amsterdam Chamber of Commerce in 1976 to confirm that Greg was authorised to use the Magic Bus name and had been *"operating independently"* from his own organisation since 1 August 1975. A good friend.

The Tiger's Tale & Other Stories

Nee told me many interesting stories in 2025:

"I vividly remember transporting a young tiger from a barn in Amsterdam to a zoo in Wasenaar. He did figure eights in his cage all the way there, and when we arrived he was wheeled in his cage past the enclosure with the other big cats, so there was a snarling and carrying-on that was ferocious. He ended up in solitary, last seen digging furiously down to get out of the cage".

After the office was established it became easier to take money for fares in advance, but before that it was done on the bus:

"Departures to India, Athens or Istanbul were lengthy, sorting out currencies and collecting the money. Forty or fifty passengers had a lot of luggage to stow and attracted a lot of attention".

"I always gave a little speech about not being able to carry hashish over the border to Germany and that if anyone wanted they could give it to me. Then I would walk down the aisle and collect!"

"After loading at Museumplein became too public and attracted too much attention we didn't tell passengers where the bus was leaving from until departure day, when they had to 'check-in' to find out. Buses left from Oosterdock, the Rai Exhibition Center and other locations that were near tram stops. Even so, there were police who found out where the departures were, and surrounded the bus with their little VW police cars, blue lights flashing".

"They would make passengers who'd bought tickets in Amsterdam get off the bus (they had no jurisdiction over those who had bought their tickets in London). We told the banished passengers to meet us at the train station and would buy them all tickets to Haarlem or some other nearby station. The bus would depart with the passengers from London and pick up the others at the station, then off they would go to Athens, Istanbul or India".

New Beginnings

"After a while the AEC buses became too much to maintain, in addition to booking all the passengers. Gradually, owner-drivers did all the driving and maintenance, and the Magic Bus company became a booking agent, taking quite a large cut - 25% - which often caused the drivers to grumble".

Graham Bourne placed the original Rokin 24 office on the fourth floor, but it had moved to the ground floor by the time Nee returned from USA, as Greg had an arrangement to sell tickets for the local 'Circus' company tours. Magic Bus then moved to a new office on Damrak at some point in 1975, as Nee explained:

"After we moved to Damrak 87, I began to work in the office daily selling tickets and sorting out problems, 9:00 am to 6:00 pm, six days a week. There was always a huge volume of passengers, buying train tickets to London using the Olau Line from Vlissingen to Sheerness as the ferry company across the channel, and tickets by bus to Paris, Munich, Barcelona, Copenhagen, Thessalonika, Athens, Istanbul, and Delhi, and plane tickets to everywhere (a bucket shop, as they say)".

"We had three floors, train and bus on the 1st floor over the Wimpy, plane on the 2nd floor, and admin and telex on the 3rd floor. Peter Hoornweg became the office manager, and for a time he was very supportive. We had many other great people working there, selling tickets. I remember Wim Jansen, Phil Sutton, Koos Schouten, Jan Kuntkes, Ellie, and later Maarten Bolluijt".

"Many feet came up and down those stairs, which, as is typical in Amsterdam, were very steep. The telex kept us in close contact with the London, Athens and Paris offices which were the backbone of the operation. Every day would end in calculating how much money came in and depositing it by night box at the bank, which was just around the corner - one time the bag was snatched from me, but luckily the boxes were empty of money".

Shaftesbury Avenue

"I also spent a lot of time in the London office, first at 74 and then at 66 Shaftesbury Avenue, mainly working on the books. I have to say that although I am a detail person I was not brilliant at getting it right (and still have trouble balancing my checkbook). We hired a bookkeeper named Kay and she taught me a lot about it".

"I never went to any departures in London, but I did make some great friendships there, including with Karen Versteegh, Wendy Fellowes, Vivien Brodie and Helen Lipton".

Nee also remembered Tony Oliver and his sister Mandy, David Rendall and others from London (not least Barrie Moreton) as well as Rodda Thomas and others from Amsterdam.

Nee enjoyed working in the offices. The sheer volume of people coming in to buy tickets was exhausting, and the staff were usually worn out at the end of each day - but they often met up in the pub after work to wind down.

Amusingly, Nee told me that one day a phone call came in from Pete Townshend, who wanted to use the Magic Bus name for his new Richmond bookshop. *"Sure, as long as you don't sell bus tickets"* was her cheeky response.

Advertisements in Melody Maker from 1977.

Time Out

The London weekly listings magazine *Time Out* was - at least as far as I can determine - the first UK outlet that Magic Bus advertised in, starting in March 1974.

By September there were often several ads on the same page, and so it continued every week until 1982. There was plenty of competition, but the distinctive Magic Bus ads usually stood out.

Time Out was very important to Magic Bus.

On 10 January 1975 the office was in Giesbach Road and the fare to Delhi was £70, but by March the office was in Holloway Road, the fare to Delhi was £55 and the classic logo had been introduced.

I didn't buy *Time Out* myself back then - I mostly read the *Evening Standard* (where Magic Bus advertised frequently), *Melody Maker* (likewise) and *Private Eye* (which offered other buses to Kathmandu, one of which I took).

Looking through old copies now it is clear that competition was robust, but that Magic Bus had unique brand recognition.

It was surprising, though, to see some prominent Magic Bus ads that didn't give an address or telephone number, and it is hard to believe that this was not an oversight.

No address, no phone number, no sales, 12 December 1975.

The company soon got its act together, with prominent ads in the classified section - complete with an address and a phone number - appearing weekly while the business was active.

In later years advertisements included Magic Train, Magic Plane and Magic Freight, along with Magic Holidays (selling Top Deck Travel and Sundowners tickets on commission), Magic Safaris (presumably something similar involving Africa) and Super Tent (a camping equipment rental service).

Time Out — London's Living Guide

EVERY DAY YOU'LL SEE THE DUST

●**MAGIC BUS.** Overland tours to Athens and India via Istanbul from 25. Phone for brochure and info etc. 01-940 3162.
15 March 1974 - first Richmond ad

●**MAGIC BUS.** Overland to Istanbul, Athens £25. Leaving every Saturday 01-940 3162 for info.
31 May 1974 - last Richmond ad

●**MAGIC BUS.** Overland to Athens, Istanbul. £25. Leaving every Friday. 01-263 0662 for info.
19 July 1974 - first Archway ad

●MAGIC BUS AFGHANISTAN. £65. 263 0662.
●MAGIC BUS INDIA. £70. 263 0662.
●MAGIC BUS MOROCCO. £27. 263 0662.
●MAGIC BUS SCANDINAVIA. £20. 263 0662.
●MAGIC BUS AUSTRIA. £16. 263 0662.
●MAGIC BUS BEOGRADE. £19. 263 0662.
●MAGIC BUS SOUTH. 263 0662.
●MAGIC BUS DELHI. £70. 263 0662.

The 'scattergun' approach.

●MAGIC BUS HOLLAND. £9. 263 0662.
●INTERNATIONAL PASSPORT to hassle-free smoking pleasure . . . 'THE TRUCKERS' BIBLE', 75p plus 10p p&p, from Release, 1 Elgin Avenue, London W9.
●MAGIC BUS MARRAKESH. £32. 263 0662.
●MAGIC BUS SPAIN. £19. 263 0662.
●MAGIC BUS GERMANY. £14. 263 0662.

The Time Out classified Travel section was not exclusively about travel and featured other items of interest.

Magic Bus

Twice Weekly departures

AMSTERDAM	£ 7
MUNICH	£ 13
BARCELONA	£ 15
SALZBURG	£ 15
COPENHAGEN	£ 17
BEOGRAD	£ 17
MILANO	£ 17
MOROCCO	£ 19
ATHENS	£ 20
ISTANBUL	£ 25
OSLO	£ 25
DELHI	£ 70
AFRICA	from £100

Phone 01-263 0662 for details or a chat.

27 September 1974 - first box ad

FOR SALE 50lb BEST NEPALESE HASHISH £5000

All you have to do is pick it up . . . in Katmandu or any other buying port and get it to a selling port like London and you've made a fortune.
But you have to get 'BUST' first.

'BUST' is the new dope dealin' board game for adults — and it's perfectly legal. The Monopoly of a new generation — with deals, heavies and gun cards instead of houses and stations.

Find out who your real friends are — get 'BUST' and deal dope with dice.

In selected shops or through the post for £3.95 inc. (Money back guarantee). From BROTHER JERRY PRODUCTIONS, BCM BOX 5646, LONDON WC1V 6XX

But that was in the good old days...

TimeOut — London's Living Guide

EVERY DAY YOU'LL SEE THE DUST

MAGIC BUS
AMSTERDAM DAILY £10.00
PARIS £10.50
+ worldwide economy travel
74 Shaftesbury Avenue, W1.
Tel: 439 0557

KABUL £55
ISTANBUL £31
MAGIC BUS
74 SHAFTESBURY AVE,
LONDON W1.
TEL: 439 0557.

MAGIC BUS
TWICE WEEKLY WITH UNLIMITED STOPOVERS IN
ATHENS £25
ISTANBUL £37
TEHRAN £62
HERAT £68
KABUL £75
DELHI £87
66 Shaftesbury Avenue,
London W1.
Tel: 439 8471

MAGIC PLANE
TEL AVIV
For under 26 year olds
o/w £64. r/t £128
66 Shaftesbury Avenue
London W1.
439 8479

MAGIC BUS SPAIN
BARCELONA £27
ALICANTE £34
plus reductions for students and Spanish residents.
Contact: MAGIC BUS,
66 Shaftesbury Avenue,
London W1. Tel: 439 8471.

MAGIC BUS ATHENS £30.00
+ PART WAY DESTINATIONS
LONDON TO ANY STATION IN HOLLAND £10.00
74 SHAFTESBURY AVENUE
LONDON W1
TEL: 439 0557

MAGIC BUS DELHI £80
Via Paris
Contact:
74 Shaftesbury Avenue,
London W1.
Tel: 439 0729/0557

MAGIC BUS LISBON £38.50
Via Paris
Contact:
74 Shaftesbury Avenue,
London W1.
Tel: 439 0729/0557

Ads from the Shaftesbury Avenue offices 1976-1978

The AEC Buses

Graham Bourne was introduced to the Magic Bus 'fleet' soon after arriving in Beesd. A large Fiat had been bought for the India run, but Greg quickly sold it to another driver.

"To the left of the Fiat stood the other two", Bourne writes. *"According to the letters above the chrome grills they were AECs, but that kind of coachwork wasn't British".*

Bourne - who had never driven a bus before - was no expert. AEC built the chassis, while various coachbuilders did the bodywork. A 'continental' design (with the 'Alpine Lights' windows around the top) was used by some companies in Britain.

The Associated Equipment Company Limited had been founded in 1912 to do chassis-building for London buses, but during the First World War it also began to manufacture trucks.

In 1926 a new factory was built in Windmill Lane, Southall, and the company stayed there until 1979, producing buses, trucks and engines and exporting them worldwide.

For my generation AEC was best known for building London's red double-decker Routemaster buses, which served the capital from 1956 until 2005 - but an even older AEC Regal III coach, built in Southall in 1949 and driven by Paddy Garrow-Fisher, was the first to do the India run in 1957.

Greg Williams bought three used AEC coaches from a company in Zeeland in 1973. The models are not known, but photographs show that, while similar, they were not identical.

According to Bourne, one of them - which both he and Greg drove - was known as 'Little Bus', and had the company name *"painted orange in large, rounded, overlapping letters along each side"*. There was a photograph of what seemed to be it in Greg's archive.

Digging deeper, I found another bus with the same lettering, this one with *"Col d'Izoord"* also visible at the front, along with a couple who Nee identified as Gina and Tony. A much later book claimed - incorrectly - that this was *"the original Magic Bus"*.

Also in the archive was an oversized negative that I hadn't noticed at first - it was in very poor condition, but upon closer inspection it showed a barely visible bus. So I scanned it and made adjustments in a graphics editor, which revealed that it was another AEC bus, this time named *"Monte Gioveretto"*, and it also had 'Magic Bus' painted on the side in the style described by Graham Bourne, with the number plate TB-35-21.

Another archive shot showed a bus with *"Magic Bus Co"* on the destination board, though without any signwriting on the side - there did seem to be a name at the front but the photograph was low resolution and it was illegible

Nee told me that the third bus was named *"Zugspitze"*, after the highest mountain in Germany (located on the Austrian border), and that the company name was added later.

Which of these buses survived to become 'Little Bus' is unclear, but by 1975 it had been scrapped. From then on, the Magic Bus company was a booking agency only.

*This AEC bus says 'Magic Bus Co' on the destination board.
It also has the name "Zugspitze" painted at the front.*

*An AEC coach with Magic Bus painted on the side.
This one has the name "Col d'Izoord" at the front.*

Another AEC vehicle with Magic Bus painted on the side. This one has "Monte Gioveretto" written at the front.

This is thought to be "Little Bus", out on the road somewhere between Amsterdam and Athens.

Jochen Reier

Graham Bourne only once writes about smuggling contraband, and then obliquely, in a passage that mentions a return bus trip to Morocco by Greg's bus-owning friends *"Tony and Cathy"* and a nervous moment at the house in Beesd.

But Bourne also describes a visit to a large house in Munich in May 1974 - it was a city that all overland drivers on the main route stopped in, and he was guided by his co-driver Eric on the way back from Athens after his second trip.

"Fixed to one of the broken-plaster gateposts", he writes, *"hung a crudely painted sign stating, 'Vorsicht, bissige Gänse', which neither of us were able to translate"*. They soon found out the hard way that it meant *"Beware, vicious geese"*.

While Bourne's account gives his host's name as 'Joe', it was in fact Jochen Reier, whose home on Schopenhauerstrasse near the Olympic Stadium was a regular stop for some drivers (those who enjoyed a smoke, basically).

A credible source who prefers to remain anonymous - let's call him 'Dope Throat' - told me that the geese had adopted a pond on the property and were treated as honoured (if noisy and sometimes aggressive) guests. And he suggested that I look up Jochen, who he had known personally and worked for.

I had initially been sceptical - a good approach to anything about the Hippie Trail - but my source soon convinced me to investigate by displaying a deep knowledge of my youthful haunts in London - this guy was clearly on the level.

He knew Jochen Reier in 1973-4 and stayed at his large house in Munich. Greg Williams was *"a frequent visitor"*, along with other bus drivers. Reier's business interests included commercial removals locally and the delivery of German trucks and other vehicles to buyers in Afghanistan and Nepal.

Jochen Reier is celebrated as the 'architect' and the driving force behind the 1983 Peace Pagoda in Munich, a copy of a Pashupatinath pagoda carved in Nepal and shipped to Germany - along with 70 kilos of Nepalese *charas*.

His 2016 book *The Curse of the Temple* covers the story and his subsequent fugitive spell in the South Seas. Reier had apparently first travelled overland to Kathmandu in 1967, getting busted on the return journey and serving four years in a Greek prison.

The English version of Reier's website says that *"About twenty times he took the adventurous route from Germany to India and Nepal, mostly as a driver of his legendary Magic Bus"* - a claim that may have gained something in the translation. His book does say that he drove some *"Magic Bus trips to Kathmandu"* in the 1970s, but never suggests that he owned the company.

Patch Badges

At some point the company had a few patch badges made for the drivers, and there were a handful in Greg Williams' archive.

The text says *"The Original Magic Bus Co Beware of Imitations"*, and part of the design echoes a doodle amongst Greg's papers. There is also a graphic of a vehicle, but it looks more like a Land Rover than a bus to me.

*Magic Bus poster from Amsterdam
Shoes by Vincent van Gogh*

*Note the Rokin 24 address - Magic Bus moved
to Damrak 87 at some point in 1975.*

Athens

While the 'Magic Bus to India' was the most famous, the Magic Bus to Athens must surely have been the more lucrative.

A bus could shuttle back and forth from northern Europe all summer, then head for Goa in the autumn. The glorious Aegean weather on the islands peaked while the monsoon swept India. The food was great, the locals were friendly, and a cohort of western youth took a tent and camped on the beach. I did it myself - but you couldn't pitch a tent in central Athens.

The Funny Trumpet's Guest-House was a back-packer hostel on Mitropoleos where bus operators would run a booking desk, and there is a Funny Trumpet's business card in Greg Williams' archive, with a helpful map on one side and an invitation to *"come and see our tropical aquarium"* on the other.

It was one of many in the area that did deals with bus companies. A representative would man the front desk during the day, the drivers would get a free crashpad, and the passengers would stay at the hotel because the bus stopped right outside. Graham Bourne recounts how in 1974 a deal was done with Alfred's Guest House, where Kevin Buckley ran the Magic Bus operation with assistance from Jacques Muscat.

The Magic Bus Athens headquarters (complete with Kevin) later moved to 'Manos House' on Kidathineon - the bus drivers were given a 4-room section for living quarters and dropped off their passengers at the door. In spring 1975 it became the Student Inn, run by Bourne's old friend Peter Stephenson.

He wasn't employed by Magic Bus but he was an integral part of the setup, hosting proceedings at Peters Fireside Pub, a popular hangout for drivers opposite the Student Inn - *"we spent most of the time partying"*, he says (as, indeed, did everyone else).

It was all about fun. Sun, sea, sex and fun.

Magic Bus was about "illegally conveying young people back and forth in clapped-out old buses between the main capitals of Europe". (Graham Bourne)

MAGIC BUS
The "sun-run" buses – a traveller's nightmare

ATHENS £25

PLUS PART WAY DESTINATIONS.

MAGIC BUS

74 SHAFTESBURY AVE,

LONDON W1.

TEL: 439 0557

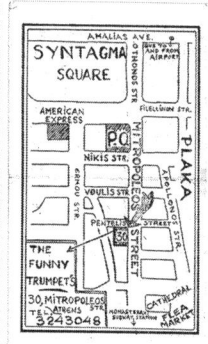

"The one doing the most business is the Magic Bus"

The pirate bus

London Evening News, 22 September 1978

Pirate Buses

The *Evening News* of 22 September 1978 ran a dramatic story by reporter Jack Aitken titled *'The Pirate Bus'*, with the strapline *"Where it leaves from nobody knows - except 50 young people on their way to adventure"*. Spooky.

The scene is set: half past three in the afternoon in the heart of London. A large group of young people hanging around, sitting on rucksacks or toting other luggage. The departure time and location had only been revealed to them the day before, and both would be different for the next day.

It's *"an elaborate cloak and dagger ritual"*, we are told. *"Suddenly a man appeared ticking off names on a clipboard"*, our intrepid man-on-the-spot reports. *"Then a coach drew up. It was of 1967 vintage and had 51 reclining seats and air conditioning"*. There is a photograph of the unbranded bus with passengers boarding. In less than five minutes it was loaded and heading for Dover.

"Another pirate bus was on its way to Greece".

The piece explains that there are *"at least a dozen pirate bus firms"* that advertised in outlets like *Time Out* and *Girl About Town*, with twenty coaches a week leaving for Athens.

"There is no way of competing with these cowboys on price while meeting the regulations of all the countries the service passes through", complains a disgruntled competitor.

As for the culprits, *"The best known and the one doing the most business is the Magic Bus, which leaves on Mondays, Tuesdays, Thursdays and Saturdays"*, we hear.

"Mr Anthony Oliver, manager of Magic Bus Tours, of Shaftesbury Avenue said: Basically we act as agents and hire the coaches. A courier boards in Belgium and stays until Athens. If any passengers get stroppy, the driver is empowered to put them off, no matter where".

The reporter gets a few vox-pops from passengers - a couple of them were heading for Nepal, but most were on their way to the Greek Islands - and he includes an unrelated interview with a previous passenger who had hated the three-day journey.

"We drove 16 hours a day", said 27-year-old Doreen Brent from Croydon. *"What with the intense heat, the constant vibration, the lack of a toilet and the fact that we were packed in like sardines, it was a terrible ordeal"*.

The article had begun as an exposé of pirate buses, but it evolved into a guide to having a cheap holiday in the Mediterranean.

Working Girls

Just take the Magic Bus to Athens, the article explains between the lines, where *"in handy proximity to the coach terminus is a cheap students' hotel"*. Then check out the job prospects in Athens and nearby resorts or head for the Greek Islands *via* Piraeus.

"A huge proportion of the thousands of Britons flocking to Greece every summer are girls on one-way tickets", the article explains. *"They travel alone or with other girls. Boy friends are considered a hindrance. And many find jobs, while at home their only prospect was the dole queue"*.

Carol Kirkwood, 19, from Clapham describes the scene:

"This is my second year in Greece. I was stoney-broke when I arrived but I had no trouble getting work as a waitress. The pay is reasonable and the tips are more than generous. When I go home next month I will go in my own car".

"It's a perfect set-up", says Carol. Sunshine in the daytime, then working at night in bars where the big spenders tipped generously. Summer days and summer nights.

Girls just wanna have fun, innit?

Chris Petropoulos

My understanding is that Greek law required foreign businesses to have a local partner, and Magic Bus Athens was founded as a separate company in which Chris Petropoulos had a share.

Chris was also the owner of Peters Fireside Pub, which had existed before Peter Stephenson arrived to help with the business.

An information sheet from 1978 says that *"Magic Bus offers a year round service to Athens and this summer we shall also be offering one way journeys to various destinations on route"*.

On Tuesdays the bus from London went *via* Paris and Stuttgart, on Thursdays *via* Frankfurt, and on Saturdays the route took in Paris, Milan and Venice. *"Trips are casual"*, the sheet says, but adds that the buses *"are not new or air-conditioned"*.

At one point Barrie Moreton was invited by Greg Williams to invest in Magic Bus Athens, with Greg, Chris and Barrie having a share each, and Barrie moving to Greece.

By this time Magic Bus had an actual office, above a dry cleaners on Kidathineon, conveniently near the Student Inn. But after a while Barrie sold his share back to Greg.

There had been friction. Barrie and Chris didn't see eye-to-eye, and Greg's long-standing and reliable agent Kevin Buckley didn't seem to figure in the new setup.

Kevin's story would offer a different perspective, and apparently some operators continued to deal with him, but I couldn't contact him for further details and must leave it there.

Eventually Chris Petropoulos set up a new office on Filellinon, as the Magic Bus company's initial pirate style was gradually left behind. Magic Bus Athens survived after the Greg Williams company collapsed, continuing in business into the 1990s.

Party Central

From its earliest days the Magic Bus company was heavily focused on Athens - it was a three-day trip from London or Amsterdam rather than the three weeks it took to get to India, it could be done more frequently, was more likely to be successful, attracted a lot more punters and generated a lot more profit.

Kevin Buckley was apparently crucial to the original setup, practical and reliable. His assistant Jacques Muscat was South African - this was problematic when travelling through Yugoslavia and I have been told he was smuggled across the borders.

Mike Newton, Fortunato and Andy Kirk

Barrie Moreton and Brodie later ran the Athens office for a while but the names that come up most frequently in online recollections are Mike Newton (who designed the t-shirts shown above), Fortunato (aka the Italian Stallion) and Andy Kirk, a 'jack-of-all-trades' who did courier trips as well as office duties.

From Funny Trumpet's to the Student Inn and Hotel California, the consistent narrative in people's reminiscences is that Athens was party central, and that the Magic Bus team, along with Peter 'The Sheriff' Stephenson, had a lot to do with it.

Undated poster from Magic Bus Athens (possibly from the 1980s post-collapse).

Note the Athens office address and the branch office address in Thessaloniki.

Istanbul

My understanding of the Magic Bus operation in Istanbul is a blurred image of a Byzantine ball of confusion wrapped inside a sweet pudding with cinnamon sprinkled on top. Or close to it.

Graham Bourne tells us that there were two competing Turkish interests - Sammy, described as *"Magic Bus's agent in Istanbul"* and the manager of the Pudding Shop, and Servet Gokkoyun from the Yeni Topkapi hotel nearby.

Bourne at this point was no longer working for Magic Bus as an employee but was an independent contractor, now driving the 'Bozo' bus for an American owner named Sam, who seems to have disliked Sammy for some reason.

"The deal is, for ten per cent Servet is going to book your passengers for Athens, and you've got a free room in the hotel", Sam explained casually. He seemed to be confident.

Bourne could foresee a potential problem though, as Servet's base was just around the corner from the Pudding Shop - but Sam was relaxed about it and just said that *"It'll keep them on their toes"* (which it apparently did).

Barrie Moreton spoke highly of Servet, who he dealt with happily for many years, including in the later 1980s when the overland route had something of a revival.

To confuse matters even further, several photographs from Greg Williams' archive show the classic Magic Bus logo used by Batu Tur in Şeftali Sokak, on the corner of Incili Çavuş Sokak - this was just around the corner from the Pudding Shop, but like other Istanbul outlets had no formal relationship with Magic Bus.

Shown a photograph, the investigative journalist Meirion Jones confirmed that he used the upstairs office while travelling back from India, and so did Dutch researcher Gerard Aartsen.

Card Trick

Carrie Cuneo wrote that her sister Susan had worked at the Magic Bus office in Istanbul saying it was *"next to the Pudding Shop"*, and other travellers tell of tickets being sold inside the Pudding Shop itself, presumably on a commission basis.

There is also an image of a business card in circulation that gives the Magic Bus Istanbul address as *"Yerebatan Cad 17/2 Sultanahmet"*, which is a little further away. No data available.

The graphic design is similar to a card used by the Athens office and the image is replicated on a t-shirt worn by one of Greg's associates in a photograph from the archive. And I have seen a photograph showing it worn by several members of the office staff from Amsterdam at an outdoor gathering.

It's all rather confusing.

Strictly Byzantine

Another shot in the archive shows the Albayrak travel agency two doors down from Batu Tur, with a sign in the window that says *"Magic Bus Istanbul"* - and Gerard Aartsen had used the company to travel from Kabul to Istanbul in March 1978.

Ten per cent was probably the going rate.

Yet another photograph in the archive almost escaped my attention, being poor quality and rather dark - it wasn't until I adjusted the brightness and contrast with a graphics editor that I realised what a piece of treasure it actually was.

It was a shop claiming to be a *"Youth and Student Travel Center"*, with a prominent Magic Bus sign. But what was actually interesting was the signwriting in the shop window next door.

"Pudding Shop Restaurant", it said.

One of the Magic Bus representatives in Istanbul was Batu Tur. This office is in Şeftali Sokak, behind the Pudding Shop.

A sign identifying Incili Çavuş Sokak is visible in this shot. The entrance to the stairs is to the left below the window.

The Albayrak travel agency also sold Magic Bus tickets. This office is in Şeftali Sokak, two doors from Batu Tur.

Susan Cuneo worked in an office "next to the Pudding Shop". Take a close look at the window on the right.

Istanbul view thought to be from 1972.

Another Istanbul office address.

Batu Tur Head Office.

Sammy & Servet

In 1974 Graham Bourne was introduced to Sammy:

"Magic Bus's agent in Istanbul was, among other questionable things, manager of a cheap cafeteria called the Pudding Shop".

Bourne describes him as having *"a face like Punch"*, along with a black Afro hairstyle and a Che Guevara t-shirt.

"He had to be one of the ugliest characters I'd ever met... I couldn't help disliking him... He also ran the only booking office in all of Turkey for the pirate buses that passed through". Sammy had four passengers for Bourne waiting outside the Pudding Shop.

"The fact that he was never caught dealing dope, exchanging monies on the black market or illegally doing business with foreign buses is because he was always tipped off in advance", says Bourne.

On a later 1974 trip Bourne was introduced to Servet Gokkoyun, the suave manager of the Yeni Topkapi hotel and another source of bookings in either direction.

One of Greg Williams' photographs from Istanbul shows a travel agent with a big Magic Bus sign next door to the Pudding Shop. Carrie Cuneo says her sister Susan worked there. Another source told me that Susan lived with Servet.

Barrie Moreton often dealt with Servet and told me that he liked to travel himself - one of the photographs of Servet in this book was taken by Barrie in Kathmandu in the late 1980s.

Apparently Servet often travelled the overland route on business - there was a good profit to be made delivering various items that were otherwise scarce to Iran, Afghanistan and Pakistan. In 2008 he told Derek Amey's *India Overland* forum that he *"continued to keep the line until 1994"*.

The Amazing Pudding

On 30 November 2020 the Dutch newspaper *De Volkskrant* ran a report from Rob Vreeken about the Pudding Shop, founded by brothers Idris and Namik Çolpan in 1957. An online translator rendered the subheading as *"Back to the legendary hippie hangout in Istanbul"*. Some more auto-translated quotes:

"The Magic Bus stopped in front of the door in the sixties".

It's quite a claim to make in the opening sentence, given that the company wasn't even founded until the 1970s. Was Cat Stevens on board? The journalist didn't ask.

"The Magic Bus stopped in front of the door twice a week", the piece continues, *"a painted Volkswagen bus with the starting point Damrak and the final stop Kathmandu"*.

A minibus from Amsterdam to Kathmandu and back in seven days. Every week, the same bus. All through the 1960s. Now that's what I would call magic (if it were true). But ace reporter Rob Vreeken doesn't seem to see any problem with it.

"The brothers even sold tickets for the Magic Bus".

The Çolpans and others sold tickets on commission for any bus - as Namik told historian Tommy Wide in January 2024, they could *"make money out of it"*. Almost everyone went to the Pudding Shop because of the innovative notice board, including drivers such as Budget Bus George, Rocket Jon Benyon and anyone else who had an empty seat to fill. It was a well-known place to arrange a ride - or pick up passengers - in either direction.

But there was no Magic Bus outside the Pudding Shop door in the 1960s, and no painted Volkswagen making weekly round trips to Kathmandu at any time. As for Cat Stevens, he is on record as saying that he never went to Kathmandu either.

Kevin Buckley at the Athens office.

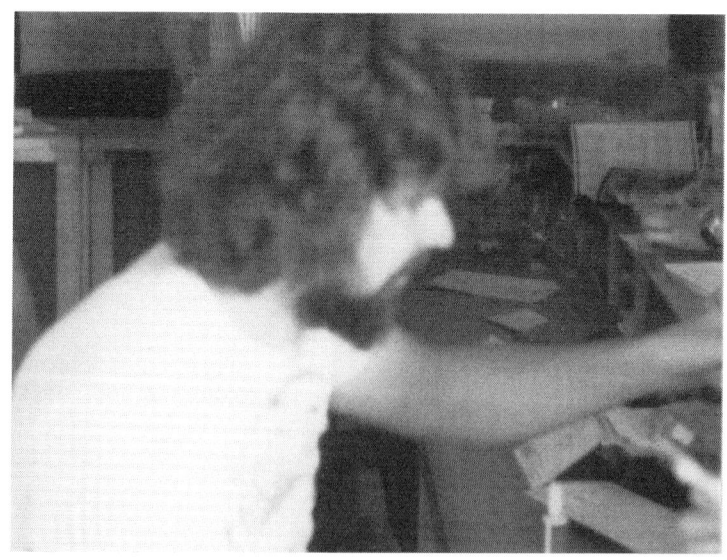

Barrie Moreton at the Athens office.

Servet Gokkoyun
Istanbul contact

Torkild Bangsbo Andersen
Copenhagen office

Pete Smith (centre) and associates.

Barrie Moreton

Barrie Moreton first went overland to India in 1966, hitching to Istanbul, driving a Mercedes to Teheran, then using the Baluchistan route. In 1967 he drove all the way in a Bedford Dormobile, and in 1968 he drove a car to India before making his way to Australia.

Barrie recalled that he first met Greg Williams in 1973 or 1974 - he had been driving minibuses on the Copenhagen-Amsterdam-Barcelona route and had offered to sell one of them to Greg (who wasn't interested). But their paths crossed many times after that, and they often did business together.

Barrie Moreton

Greg twice got Barrie involved with the Magic Bus offices, first in Athens and then in London. Barrie also drove to India for Magic Bus, and his other exploits included a tour of South America, trips across the Sahara (one escorting an Oxford University expedition), an East Africa run to Cape Town and several buses to Goa in later years. At one point he drove extensively in the USA too.

Barrie was born in King's Norton in 1944, and the Dormobile he drove to India in 1967 had previously been used by a local Birmingham band named Earth - roadie John 'Jinks' Jeffries and his brothers James and Eddie all did the India run.

In August 1969 the group, who had started out as the Polka Tulk Blues Band, changed their name again. To 'Black Sabbath'. I still have my copy of their *Paranoid* single from 1970.

I first heard of Barrie Moreton in December 2024 - I had already been researching and writing about the Magic Bus company as part of my coverage of the Hippie Trail.

Barrie saw one of my posts on a web forum and got in touch. He very quickly convinced me that he knew what he was talking about, and offered me a chance to access to the Magic Bus archive.

It was the luckiest of lucky breaks.

Misinformation

I have actually seen a document online which claims that on his first overland journey to the east Greg Williams drove *"with his Dutch partner Nee from London to New Delhi, very likely in 1969 or 1970. The vehicle: a 20-seater Ford with the words 'Magic Bus, Europe - Asia' on the side"*.

But Nee is American, she never went to Delhi, the vehicle was a Morris and she only travelled on it westbound in 1972. The source also claims that the Hippie Trail started in 1968 and that a history of the Magic Bus company is *"no longer possible"*.

Cluelessness abounds.

There is good photographic evidence of long-haired pot-smokers in Kathmandu in 1965. And if a history of the Magic Bus company were no longer possible then you are reading the wrong book.

Copenhagen

All land routes to and from Norway, Sweden and Finland to the rest of western Europe passed through Copenhagen, which had its own thriving counterculture, most famously at Christiania.

Rainbow Travel was set up by Copenhagen Barry, who settled in the city in late 1974, opening an office at Magstraede 10, which fed into the informal Magic Bus network.

Barry had known Greg Williams as a teenager and had introduced both Graham Bourne and Peter Stephenson to Magic Bus, but he was always an independent operator.

And the two old friends didn't always see eye-to-eye. Barry told me they had a falling out at the end of summer 1974, after which he moved to Copenhagen and started Rainbow Travel - Barry preferred to do business in Amsterdam with Sunshine Travel where possible, but Magic Bus could be hard to avoid.

Barry decided to bypass Amsterdam by pioneering a new route from Copenhagen *via* the Gedser ferry to Rostock and on to Berlin. At the time West Berlin was an isolated enclave surrounded by communist East Germany, with transit roads from West Germany and Scandinavia. Traffic was closely monitored.

Western vehicles were restricted in where they could stop - the fear was that they would help locals escape. But a bus could enter West Berlin on a road from the north or west, pick up passengers, then leave on the road south, eventually joining the main route in Munich and heading for Athens or Istanbul.

Barry did do business with Magic Bus a few more times, but he described the last occasion in 1978 as *"a catastrophe"*. When Barry shut up shop in 1979 his regular driver Torkild Bangsbo Andersen was engaged by Greg to run a Magic Bus operation, with Torkild also responsible for an office in Hamburg.

Torkild Bangsbo Andersen

From 1971 Torkild Bangsbo Andersen worked as a Copenhagen city bus driver for a few years before he got involved with Rainbow Travel, doing occasional trips to Amsterdam.

He had been driving buses on the Copenhagen-Amsterdam route when he first met Greg Williams in 1974, and he appears briefly in Graham Bourne's book, mentioned as co-driver with John Moore when they all met up in Istanbul.

Torkild drove several buses overland to India and Nepal in the 1970s, working for Magic Bus, Rainbow Travel and also for Amsterdam's Sunshine Travel. Respect.

Torkild didn't care for British buses - other drivers have told me the same - and spoke highly of the Setra S12 with a Henschel engine that he drove, also praising the Mercedes 321.

At my prompting Torkild listed a few of the drivers he remembered: *"Spacey Pete, Cowboy Jeff, Obnoxious Barrie, French Gerard, Dutch Gerard"* and one named *"Odd Boye"* - apparently 'Odd' is a fairly common Norwegian male forename (from the Old Norse meaning 'sharp end of an arrow' or 'edge of a blade').

In Kathmandu Torkild parked the bus in Basantapur, and on at least one trip stayed at the Yin Yang hotel. In Kabul he remembered the giant chess board at Sigi's and more: *"If I wanted a beer I usually went to The Little Lantern, a nice quiet pub run by a German lady who was married to an Afghan who taught engineering at Kabul technical university"*. How times have changed.

Torkild told me that the buses were advertised in the Danish press - regularly in *Information*, and on Tuesdays in the travel section of *Politiken*. Both were daily newspapers.

I was unable to source any examples. *Mea culpa*.

Torkild Bangsbo Andersen

Hamburg

Torkild was also responsible for the Magic Bus Hamburg office, which started out on Kleiner Burstah in a former ladies' fashion shop with pink wallpaper (soon painted over). The office later moved to other premises just north of the university.

Torkild told me that he attended a staff conference in early 1980 at a hotel near Munich: *"Attendees were from Amsterdam, London, Paris, Munich and Athens"*, he says, as the Magic Bus operation had expanded to the point where such meetings were useful.

According to Torkild, the last Magic Bus to set out for India from Copenhagen was driven by *"Gerard Wantenaar (aka Dutch Gerard, aka The Flying Dutchman)"*.

Transition

Graham Bourne's book covers a period in which Magic Bus begins as a fledgling company without an office that owned a handful of buses and employed several drivers. By the end of the book there are offices in Amsterdam and London and the Magic Bus business model is on the way to becoming that of a regular travel agent.

Bourne's 562-page volume records about nine months. It is the only account of the Magic Bus company that I have ever heard of and must be seen as a primary source, but Bourne was a driver - not a company insider - and largely peripheral.

Graham Bourne doesn't mention Nee anywhere.

He wasn't privy to any actual business matters, spent most of his time shuttling between Amsterdam, Athens and Istanbul, and very quickly became an independent contractor - just one of many drivers who did tours for Magic Bus, and one of the very few in the early days who never actually set foot in Asia.

I haven't seen the other two volumes of the *Bourne Chronicles* as my attempts to contact members of his family went nowhere. The books have been described elsewhere as *"self indulgent"*.

Bereavement

Greg Williams' mother Pauline died on 10 June 1974.

Graham Bourne (who probably knew nothing about it) says that Greg flew to England in May that year and again in the summer, and it seems likely that he made the trip fairly often anyway, on business or otherwise.

Greg Williams' archive also contains a copy of a will left by his paternal grandmother Jenny, dated 11 November 1975, in an envelope addressed to him at Nieuwendijk, which includes *inter alia* a bequest to Greg and any children he may have.

The Hippie Trail

Apart from a clearly false claim in *Algemeen Dagblad* in 1972 - that Greg Williams *"has already been to Nepal and back three times this year with this bus"* - I have seen no evidence that the original painted Magic Bus ever went to Kathmandu.

We do know that it went to Delhi and back that year, but there is no trace of it reaching Nepal - Nee was sceptical when I asked her, and it seems that Greg never spoke about the country.

Magic Bus did offer later trips to Nepal - I have seen advertisements from 1975 onwards, and numerous independent contractors are known to have done the journey (some of them several times).

Kathmandu was famously the end of the Hippie Trail, originally called the Hashish Trail in 1967, with the main destinations being Afghanistan and Nepal (where the best *hashish* came from) and Goa (where the beaches and party scene were the attraction).

Kabul, the capital of Afghanistan, was popular with hippies, often listed as a destination by Magic Bus. Its most famous hangout was Sigi's Hotel & Restaurant - Tony Wheeler, Rory MacLean, David Tomory, Wikipedia and others will tell you that it was on Chicken Street, but they are all clueless.

Nee told me that she visited Sigi's in 1972. Judy Casselden, aged 17, stayed there in 1973. And yours truly, aged 18, ate there many times in 1974. Sigi's wasn't on Chicken Street but was a brisk five minute walk away on what Google Maps now calls Sulh Road.

In Kathmandu the hippies headed for Freak Street. The notorious *hashish* shops were closed in July 1973 but the scene continued, with *hashish* still available and openly smoked in chillums.

The 'experts' all say that Cat Stevens wrote songs in Kathmandu in 1969, but they are clueless about that too - the man himself told a journalist in 1972 that he'd never been there.

*Sigi's Hotel & Restaurant in Kabul.
Founded by and named after Siegfried Zuern,
it continued under his business partner Jabhoor
after Sigi returned to Germany in 1972.*

Photograph by Richard Gregory.

66 Shaftesbury Avenue, London W.1.
01 439 8471 · Telex 21194

Chapter 4
THE TRAVEL AGENT

Main Offices in: London·Amsterdam·Paris·Athens

Kamer van Koophandel en Fabrieken voor Amsterdam
Koningin Wilhelminaplein 13 Amsterdam 1017

dossier nr. 143.950.-
vervolgvellen: geen.-

Uittreksel uit het Handelsregister

van de eenmanszaak: INTERNATIONAL PULLMAN.--
Zaakadres: Amsterdam-C, Damrak 87.--

Ingeschreven: 19 december 1975.--
Tijdstip van vestiging: 1 augustus 1975.--

Bedrijf: reisbemiddelingsbureau.--

Eigenaar:

Gregory WILLIAMS, wonende: Londen W.1, Engeland, Shaftesbury Avenue 74, geboren te Bristol, Engeland, 6 maart 1950, nationaliteit Britse.--

Gevolmachtigde:

Peter Anton Marie HOORNWEG, wonende te Amsterdam, Houtrijkstraat 158, geboren te Den Haag, 10 april 1951, nationaliteit Nederlandse.-

Inhoud der volmacht: betrokkene heeft algehele volmacht.---

Er worden tevens zaken gedaan onder de handelsnamen:
INTERNATIONAL MAGIC BUS; INTERNATIONAL MAGIC PLANE; INTERNATIONAL MAGIC BOAT; INTERNATIONAL MAGIC TRAIN; INTERNATIONAL MAGIC TRAVEL.--

Amsterdam, 20 AUG. 1976
voor uittreksel

The Magic Bus company was formally registered in Holland as International Pullman on 19 December 1975, stating that it had been operating since 1 August that year. In theory it had previously been part of the Amsterdamse Mobiel Straet Circus Company de Magic Bus, with which it shared an office address at Rokin 24.

Company Registrations

A document in the archive shows that Greg Williams registered the name International Pullman in Holland on 19 December 1975, claiming to have established the business on 1 August that year and to also be using other names including International Magic Bus, International Magic Plane, International Magic Boat and International Magic Train.

Peter Hoornweg is named as *"Authorised representative"* and the business address is given as Damrak 87 (Greg's address is given as 74 Shaftesbury Avenue, the London office at the time).

Another document confirms that the company had been *"operating independently from de stichting de Amsterdamse Mobiel Straet Circus Company de Magic Bus since August 1, 1975"*.

Torkild Bangsbo Andersen confirmed that International Pullman was the name registered in Denmark (and probably elsewhere), while Chris Petropoulos registered International Pullman Greece Ltd. But there is little known about the UK operation.

Magic Bus later became a limited company registered in England, *'The Magic Bus Travel Company Limited'*. I know this because the notice to creditors after the company went bust is available in a public archive - but the incorporation date is not given.

A *Lanarkshire Sunday Post* piece on 7 August 1983 titled *'The Sad Tale Of The Magic Bus'* dealt with the company's demise: *"Inquiries show Magic Bus was set up in the 60s and turned into a limited company in October 1982"*, it said.

I couldn't find any official confirmation, but that date is only a few weeks before the firm went bust on 24 December 1982 - and Companies House records that the successor *'Magic Bus Travel Company (1983) Limited'* was actually incorporated on the day before the collapse. It all seems distinctly murky.

Marketing

The success of the Magic Bus company was undoubtedly due to word of mouth to some extent in the early days - in pre-internet times the 'underground' network could be surprisingly effective. But the key - in Britain, at least - was press advertising.

Anyone wanting to travel would probably consult the classified ads in the popular press to see the options available - London's *Evening Standard* was an obvious source for those in the capital, as was *Time Out,* which was a dedicated listings magazine.

Magic Bus advertised heavily in both, and to a lesser extent in other publications such as *The Guardian, The Observer,* and *The Times.* But there were also ads in some of the provincial papers and in the *Melody Maker* and *New Musical Express* too.

Reading Evening Post 1975 and London Evening Standard 1979.

I have seen very few examples of advertising on the continent. The main exception comes from a local weekly newsletter in Amsterdam called *Use It* from June 1976, preserved in Greg Williams' archive - four sides of A4, published by 'Commissie Jeugdtoerisme' and mostly in English. It is not exactly mainstream, though I am told that Magic Bus did use small ads in the Dutch press.

Torkild Bangsbo Andersen mentioned ads in the Danish press and I would expect to find some examples in the French and German papers if I had access and a better command of the languages.

One way or another, word got around - and not just in Europe.

New York Times

On 18 July 1976 the *New York Times* ran an article titled *A Budget Bus Trip Across Europe*, in which Rod Townley and his friend Steve take a trip from London to Istanbul at the end of winter.

The Budget Bus company was not involved: *"Travel agents I talked to in America returned a blank look when I asked about bus travel across Europe. They'd heard of Europabus ($147, one way, from London to Athens), but less expensive lines such as Magic Bus, Sundowner's, Consulis, Unal or European Express (the company we are signed up with and whose bus we will board in Belgium) were unknown to them. Yet, short of hitchhiking, there is no cheaper way to travel"*.

That is the only mention of the Magic Bus company in the piece, but there are many similarities, including a shuttle service from Victoria to Dover, an English courier, and Greek drivers who pilot the actual bus from Zeebrugge.

The first toilet stop is at the German border, where some of the gentlemen passengers are asked to push-start the vehicle (a regular occurrence). The bus breaks down in Yugoslavia. It is heading for Athens, and when Rod and Steve disembark at Thessaloniki they find that Steve's suitcase has been lying in a pool of water for three days and the contents largely ruined.

In Istanbul they meet travellers on the Kathmandu run, including the redoubtable Mr Latif, *"a Hindu with a kindly, all-suffering face"*, the owner of Intercontinental Transits, a company based at 184 Goldhawk Road, Shepherd's Bush.

The original driver had quit in Austria for some reason, which required Mr Latif to fly out and drive the rest of the way himself. The bus had already broken down in Greece, we are told, *"and one of his passengers, a young New Jerseyan named Veronica, hitched to a nearby town for a tow truck"*.

Magic Bus was unique in some ways. But only some.

The *New York Times* was at it again on 10 July 1977 with an article titled *What's Doing in Istanbul* by Steven V and Cokie Roberts.

"Near the Blue Mosque in the Old City of Istanbul, there are two signs taped to the window of the Magic Bus Company. One advertises a bus leaving at 5 pm for Teheran, Kabul and New Delhi; the other, bus an hour later for Athens, Munich and London".

Once again, that is the only mention of Magic Bus - the piece is otherwise an examination of the tourist attractions of Istanbul, aimed at those who might stay at the Hilton or the Sheraton.

The article is certainly unusual in not name-checking the famous Pudding Shop. But it does clearly illustrate how well-known the Magic Bus company was in the 1970s.

Z-Plates

Vehicles sold in Germany for export were given oval 'Z Plates' (the Z is for 'Zoll' aka 'Customs Duty') - but once they left the country they were not allowed back in without the full tax being paid.

Bus drivers would buy a newish model at auction, perhaps branded to a firm that had gone bust, use it in southern Europe for the summer, then head for Goa or Kathmandu in the autumn, selling the bus in Asia and flying back to Europe.

Alan Henderson

Alan Henderson first drove a tour for Magic Bus in January 1976 with his brother John, a regular Magic Bus contractor who did three trips to India. Alan remembered visiting the Holloway Road office and alerted me to the company's *Time Out* listings.

Alan never did the India run himself but did drive the London to Athens route for Magic Bus, as well as other destinations including Venice. He also remembered visiting the next company office after the move to 74 Shaftesbury Avenue.

He told me that he once visited the Amsterdam flat over the shops at Nieuwendijk with his wife Flora before going out for dinner with Greg and Nee - he also said that Nee gave him the nickname 'Whippersnapper' (and he seemed rather proud of it).

In London he picked up his Magic Bus passengers in the street somewhere near Victoria Coach Station (but not inside it), while in Amsterdam he generally used the Oosterdock car park near the main railway station.

Alan Henderson explained to me that bus drivers often carried more than one passport - because these filled up very quickly when you drove across international borders for a living, and you had to keep ordering new ones.

This may have had other advantages, of course - any details entered into one passport might conveniently be absent from the other. God bless Hooky Street.

Alan remembered Greg Williams using a rope to get a bus started in the street (while clearly enjoying it), and mentioned fellow drivers Scottish Bob, Spacey Pete and Fat Roger.

The Last Waterhole in Amsterdam was a popular driver hangout, while the Egg Cream café (opposite Sunshine Travel) was their preferred venue for breakfast. Drivers cared about breakfast.

Carrie Cuneo

She wasn't the only female bus driver on the road to Kathmandu, but Carrie Cuneo seems to have been the only one to offer any testimony. It's very short, accompanied by several photographs from her trips, and I found it posted online in 2021:

"From November 1975 through December 1977, I made several trips to India and Nepal with Magic Bus. I traveled as a passenger on my first trip then was a bus driver on three more trips from Europe to Asia. I drove to Nepal only during the fall and winter, the cooler months, and spent summers driving in Europe. For the voyages East, I picked up my passengers from Amsterdam, Athens or Istanbul as well as other stops along the way. My sister, Susan Cuneo, worked in the Magic Bus office in Istanbul, next to the Pudding Shop. The drives from Holland to Kathmandu took 4-5 weeks, depending upon weather, road conditions, passengers or border-crossing hassles. These excursions were ideal for the more independent traveler since passengers could get on or off as they wished. My trips were one-way only as I sold my buses in Nepal and flew back to Europe. Each trip was a unique adventure".

Barrie Moreton told me that he had met Carrie on the road on his travels a few times. *"She was a nice lass"*, he recalled.

Magic Bus Logo

In 1977 Magic Bus often had three box ads on the same page in *Time Out*, each one with a different logo, and none of them the classic one - that logo, current research suggests, first appeared in March 1975 but after early 1976 it wasn't used again in *Time Out* until November 1978 for some reason.

No details are known of the logo's designer. Greg Williams' archive does contain some doodles, artist unknown, one of which was the basis of the signwriting on Little Bus (and another inspired the drivers' patch badge), but none bear any relation to the classic.

The design uses a Cooper Black font, as does the picture sleeve for the 1968 single issued by The Who - whether this was just a coincidence is impossible to say, and I would also be very wary of suggesting that the litigious Stelios of easyJet (and more recently easyBus) was inspired by the Greg Williams brand.

There are many variations on the classic Magic Bus logo, some of them crudely drawn - I have seen Magic Train, Magic Plane, Magic Inn and Magic Ski (though not Magic Freight).

My favourite is the one on the company letterhead, which uses non-italic Cooper Black in outline, seen nowhere else.

Artwork

I have been unable to discover who was responsible for the Magic Bus artwork, which ranged from the design of the classic logo (which was introduced in 1975) to the various t-shirts seen over the years, the murals at the New Oxford Street office and the graphic design and cartoon images in the *Time Out* advertisements and elsewhere.

There may have been more than one person involved, but while I can't give them the credit they deserve I can at least show examples of the work they produced. Respect.

CLASSIFIED

MAGIC BUS TRAVEL
LONDON-AMSTERDAM £9·00
14 departures every week
by British Rail, luxurious
Danish Ferry, Dutch Rail.
SINGLE : £9·00
RETURN : £17·50
01-272 5553
637 Holloway Road, N.7
(Archway Tube)

Magic Bus — Magic Plane
South of France £30 single,
£50 return; Paris £11.50;
Amsterdam £12; Dublin
(Dun Laoghaire) £22 return.
Regular departures to:
Athens £38, Hamburg £24,
Copenhagen £31, Munich £26,
Strasbourg £21.
ULTRA LOW FARES WORLD WIDE
Bus enquiries: 01-439 8475
Plane enquiries: 01-439 8479
or to book call into 66 Shaftesbury Ave, London W1.

Magic Bus

Hectic young travel office seeks ticketing staff. Languages/travel/office experience necessary. Salary negotiable.

Ring Dave on 01-439 8475
Magic Bus,
66 Shaftesbury Ave., W1

MAGIC BUS
urgently requires
MAGIC PERSON
to work in their hectic London office. Travel and office experience essential, some typing and languages a plus. Salary negotiable.
'Phone 01-439 8475

MAGIC BUS
Starting December 5th. New daily coach services to DUBLIN. £10 only. Phone (01) 439 8471 or call into 66 Shaftesbury Avenue, W1.

MAGIC BUS overland to Athens, Istanbul £25.00p leaving every Saturday. Phone 01-263 0662 for details—right on!

International Times, 1 July 1974

AMSTERDAM daily from £10.00
PARIS £10.00
ATHENS £30.00
BARCELONA £22.00
ALICANTE £34.00
DELHI £80.00
MOROCCO £47.00
66 SHAFTESBURY AVENUE, LONDON W1
TEL: 01 439 0729/0557

BEACHQUEST

The different camping tour.
Three weeks, 7 countries.

Just £100 departs 29.7.78.

66 Shaftesbury Avenue,
London W1.
Phone 439 8471

MAGIC BUS
are looking for an experienced Ledger Clerk to work in its new Oxford St. office. Salary £4500. Tel. 01-836 4670.

CLASSIFIED

Magic Bus

ATHENS
£25 o.w. (£50 return)
3 times weekly in luxury, air-conditioned coaches with reclining seats.

also **DELHI £82**
with unlimited stopovers in
ISTANBUL £37.00
TEHRAN £57.00
KABUL £70.00
66 Shaftesbury Avenue, London W1
439 8471

Magic Bus

AMSTERDAM AND PARIS	
DAILY	£10.00
ATHENS	£25.00
BARCELONA	£26.00
DELHI	£70.00
MOROCCO	£47.00

WORLDWIDE TRAVEL AT ECONOMY RATES.

CONTACT: 74 SHAFTESBURY AVE., LONDON W.1
TEL: 01-439 0729 / 0557

DAMRAK 87
22·32·42
24·10·21

BOOKKEEPER
Top-class BOOKKEEPER for busy young travel agency; must be able to do accounts to trial balance and work under own initiative; plenty of responsibility for the right person; salary negotiable. Write and tell us about yourself. MAGIC BUS, 66 Shaftesbury Avenue, London W1V 7DF.

Magic Bus presents~ BEACHQUEST CAMPING TOURS~ *

Left: Scottish Bob Turton and passenger   Right: Driver Spacey Pete

In bed with Peter 'The Sheriff' Stephenson
All photographs by Barrie Moreton.

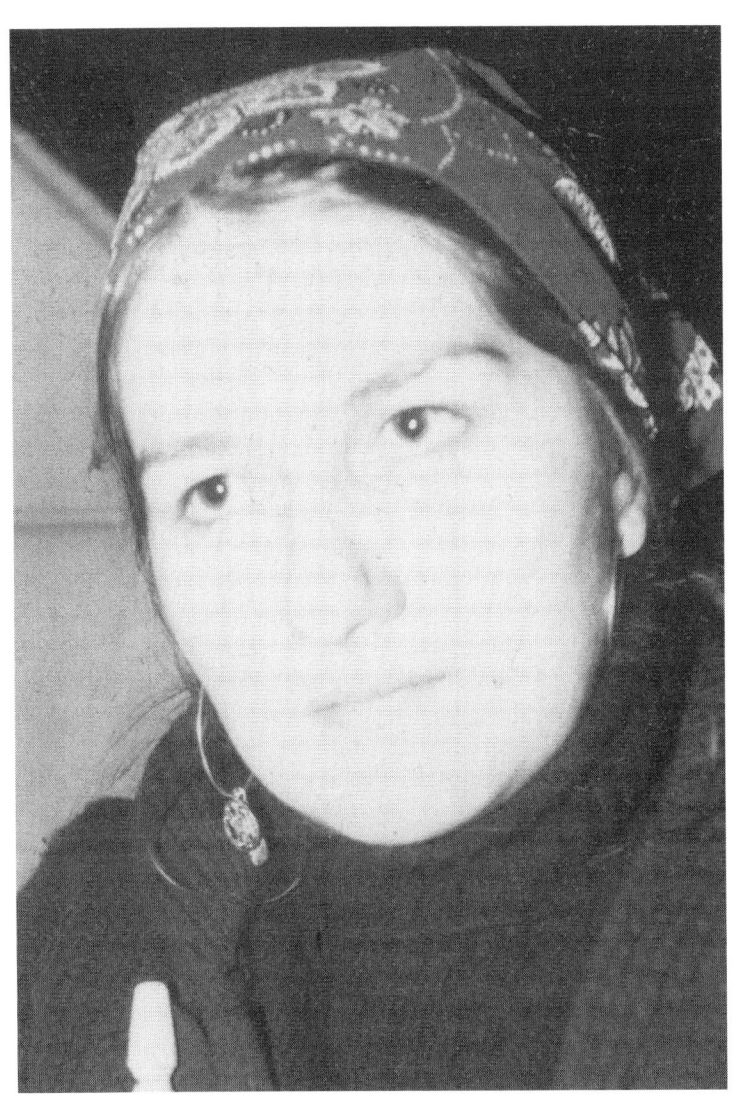

Karen Versteegh
Karen ran the first proper London office
in Holloway Road and later initiated
the move to Shaftesbury Avenue.
Photograph by Barrie Moreton.

Office Moves

By December 1975 the Magic Bus Amsterdam office at Rokin 24 had moved to Damrak 87 - Alan Henderson told me it was above a Wimpy Bar (subsequently confirmed by others).

The London office moved by June 1976 from 637 Holloway Road to 74 Shaftesbury Avenue, a much better location, apparently at the instigation of office manager Karen Versteegh - many other travel firms had offices in the area, some on the same block.

Meanwhile in Athens things were being put on a more business-like footing, with an office at Kidathineon 24 above a dry-cleaners run by Kevin Buckley with assistance from Jacques Muscat, Mike Newton, Andy Kirk and Fortunato (with Chris Petropoulos as the necessary Greek partner).

Istanbul, as we have seen, was something of a free-for-all, with many offices springing up claiming to be agents or representatives - it seems that they all sold tickets on a commission basis and Greg Williams was not involved in running them, though he preferred to work with Servet Gokkoyun.

Business was brisk and the company was growing fast. Despite a decidedly shaky start, Magic Bus was becoming a success.

Wedding

Cornelia Gaines and Greg Williams were married on 27 March 1976 in her home town of Darien, Connecticut, with Reverend Samuel W Fogel presiding. The ring cost $98.98 and the licence was five bucks, according to documents in the archive.

It should not be forgotten that Nee was actually a co-founder of the Magic Bus company, *"driving a desk"* at offices in Amsterdam and London and tempering Greg's wilder ideas. She resigned her position with the company in February 1980 and the divorce was finalised the next year.

Household Name

By September 1977 the London office had moved a few doors down to 66 Shaftesbury Avenue and the company had established itself as a household name in England.

Some ads in the press were now of the *'Staff Wanted'* variety as the business expanded, offering new services such as Magic Train, Magic Plane, and even Magic Freight.

It also introduced the new 'Beachquest' tours, mostly camping out around Europe in the summer on a cheap round trip but also offering Beachquest in Morocco.

There was something for everyone.

On 14 June 1978 the *Liverpool Daily Post* ran a full-page piece with the title *'Magic, the bus that goes to India'* - there is a copy preserved in the archive.

Greg Williams is described as a pioneer *"who drove his own bus to India six or seven years ago"*, while Capricorn Travels, Encounter Overland and Trail Finders also get a plug.

Sarah Carruthers at the Magic Bus London office tells us that they didn't sell return tickets for the India run because the drivers stayed as long as they wanted - *"but there are a lot of buses coming back and you can always find one in the big bus park at Connaught Circus"*.

"Magic Bus charges £87 for a one-way five-week trip to Delhi", the journalist Alison Maitland tells us, adding that *"Magic Bus takes a lot of Australians and New Zealanders, Dutch, Americans and French, as well as a few English people"*.

This was the peak year of the 'Magic Bus to India'. While the hippies themselves had already fallen out of fashion, the Hippie Trail had become a well-trodden 'rite of passage' for western youth. But all good things come to an end.

The Route Of All Evil

Alan Henderson was driving his own coach on a private contract through Iran in November 1978, carrying a group of Christians from Kent - they were returning from a trip to Abadan, an ancient city on the Gulf with a historic Armenian community.

In September the Shah's army had shot dead a number of protesters in Teheran's Jaleh Square - various figures have been given, but the rumour on the street was that *"thousands have been massacred by Zionist troops"*. It was the beginning of the Iranian revolution.

A general strike followed, shutting down the oil industry and plunging the country into strife, and on 5 November 1978 the British Embassy in Teheran was attacked and set ablaze.

Alan Henderson and his passengers, who had arrived in Tabriz seeking exit visas, were told these could only be issued in Teheran - but with no telex working and the burning embassy shown on television he eventually got permission to head for the Turkish border and relative safety.

It was a sign of things to come - the Shah fled in January 1979 and Ayatollah Khomeini returned from exile on 1 February, beginning the change to an Islamic Republic. Zealots were known to attack symbols of western influence, including cinemas and shopping centres. The situation was tense.

The *Associated Press* posted a report on 11 February: *"In one of its first acts, the Provisional Operational Staff of the Islamic Revolutionary Movements closed Iran's borders and all airports for 24 hours beginning Monday, Tehran Radio said"*.

It was only a 24-hour closure as stated, and the road was open again the next day - though Rory MacLean later converted this into *"one of the first actions of Khomeini's Revolutionary Council in 1979 was to close the [hippie] trail"*, one of many reasons why his *Magic Bus* book should not be taken seriously.

Afghanistan

Despite local tensions, buses continued to cross Iran in transit, and most of them also passed through Afghanistan - the route to India was significantly shorter and the roads were much better than the southern passage *via* Baluchistan.

Plus, of course, for the actual hippies on the actual Hippie Trail, the country was an actual destination - I had a great time in Herat, Kandahar and Kabul on the way out, and deliberately spent more time in the country on the way back.

Photographs by Cornelia Gaines 1972.

It may seem difficult to believe in the 21st century, but during the Hippie Trail era of the 1960s and 1970s we found the Afghans to be friendly and fun - the men and boys, that is. Women had more freedom than they do now, though only in the main cities and still with strict limits imposed. There was progress, at least.

But now Afghanistan was having a different revolution.

The Russians Are Coming

Afghanistan was a major attraction on the Hippie Trail, and Magic Bus ads often gave the price to Kabul, a popular destination.

When the Afghan king Zahir Shah was deposed in July 1973 by his cousin Mohammed Daoud few westerners noticed - it was over very quickly and almost bloodless, while Daoud was a former prime minister. In some ways it was an internal dispute.

But the Saur Revolution of April 1978 was different - Daoud, who had made himself president and got his picture on the banknotes, was brutally killed, along with most of his family.

Wikipedia says a member of the former royal family, Ali Abdul Seraj, was also due to be executed but escaped with his wife and child *"while disguised as a hippie, joining a bus full of British and Australian hashish smokers"*. The citation leads nowhere.

For the average Afghan, the revolution was no laughing matter - resistance was savagely repressed and many were apparently executed. Guerilla movements formed in response.

Emil Bryden of Budget Bus had driven through Afghanistan many times over the previous decade, and told me that the change was noticeable on his last return in 1979 - the new government was attempting to impose itself, and the tension was obvious.

A 1982 piece in *The Guardian* about the later collapse of Magic Bus began with the claim that *"the company which beat the Russians in Afghanistan and the Ayatollah in Iran has finally fallen foul of an old-fashioned capitalist cash crisis"*.

But the Magic Bus company did not engage with, let alone beat, any Iranian clerics or Russians, so it's a mystery how the journalist got the idea. And the terrible truth had actually been published in *The Guardian* on 13 September 1979.

A Magic Bus from Istanbul with a Turkish driver had ignored the advice to travel in convoy, and 45 minutes out of Herat the bus was attacked. Canadian Gaeton Dion and Kurt Marfurt of Switzerland were killed, and others were seriously injured.

The overland Hippie Trail was coming to an end.

Penny Junor

One of the few press cuttings kept in Greg Williams' archive is a piece by Penny Junor in her *'Shopping Precinct'* column - the publication and date are not identified, but the content clearly indicates that it is from September 1979.

"Beware of the Magic Bus Company, which advertises trips to India... The last people I heard of who went on one of these magical tours were attacked by bandits in Afghanistan; two of their friends were shot dead and two more severely injured".

Penny relates how the tour had set out on 1 September 1979 from Istanbul - the passengers had been assured that they would bypass Afghanistan, by then considered too dangerous. But the driver, who she implies had lucrative business there, changed the route.

Some passengers wanted to get off but were refused a refund. The bus set out from Herat and was ambushed by gunmen.

"The driver fled; so with two dead and three injured, one of the passengers drove the bus back to Herat... 26 of the passengers chartered a plane to Kabul... Those who couldn't afford it are possibly still in Herat, waiting for someone to drive the bus".

As for Magic Bus liability, *"It appears they don't have a registered office in Turkey - where all the tickets were issued - but sub-contract to a very small firm called Otulu Tours".*

Magic Bus never went through Afghanistan again.

Hounded to Afghanistan

Beware of the Magic Bus Company, which advertises trips to India. The last people I heard of who went on one of these magical tours were attacked by bandits in Afghanistan; two of their friends were shot dead and two more severely injured.

Not that the Magic Bus Company can be held responsible for bandits. What they *can* be held responsible for, however, is taking tourists through Afghanistan when they were strongly advised not to, and when all 44 passengers said they didn't want to risk it.

The tour had set out from Instanbul on 1 September, bound for Delhi. When the passengers bought their tickets from Magic Bus in Istanbul, they were told the bus would go through Iran and Pakistan; but just before departure they were told there was good news from Afghanistan and it would now be possible to go through that country instead.

When they reached Tehran, just to be on the safe side, the passengers decided to check the situation in Afghanistan with their respective embassies. All of them were strongly advised not to cross the border.

All 44 passengers told the driver they wanted to go via the original route and not through Afghanistan. The driver flatly refused and said it would be impossible to take the bus through Pakistan anyway because it had a long wheelbase and wasn't equipped for the journey.

Some of the passengers decided to get off, and asked the driver for a refund. He refused, so they all sat tight and went on into Afghanistan.

On the second day, travelling between Herat and Kabul, they were attacked by bandits in the mountains. The driver fled; so with two dead and three injured, one of the passengers drove the bus back to Herat, but it was too dangerous to go any further. Friends of the injured stayed with them and bought drugs etc; 26 of the passengers chartered a plane to Kabul (at 76 dollars each) and carried on alone from there. Those who couldn't afford it are possibly still in Herat, waiting for someone to drive the bus.

The Magic Bus Company, meanwhile, haven't paid a bean, and can't be held responsible for compensation. It appears they don't have a registered office in Turkey — where all the tickets were issued — but sub-contract to a very small firm called Otulu Tours. The only person from whom they might have got a refund was the driver.

But what, I wonder, could have made the driver so keen to take the bus through Afghanistan when everyone knew it was so dangerous?

Each passenger paid about £40 for the trip, which comes to a total of £1,760 in fares. Yet the driver admitted that he was being paid more than £3,000 for the Istanbul-Delhi run.

PENNY JUNOR

Greg Williams didn't preserve many press cuttings in his archives, but he did keep this one about the September 1979 disaster in Afghanistan when two passengers were shot dead.

The Magic Bus never went to Kabul again.

Magic Bus Afghani Ambush

'We'll take you almost anywhere,' say the advertisements for Magic Bus, the low-cost, international travel firm, spawned from the old hippie ideal of cheap-freak travel. At the end of last month, two of Magic Bus's passengers went possibly a little further than they had intended - they were killed in an ambush in Afghanistan.

Now Magic Bus, whose headquarters are in Shaftesbury Avenue, are warning prospective travellers that it is no longer possible to guarantee their journeys to the Far East. It means that the cheapest, if perhaps not the most comfortable, method of travelling East is under threat.

The ambush took place shortly after the bus had left Herat near the Iranian border, en route for Kabul and Khandahar. Because there have recently been frequent incidents of traditionalist tribal guerillas attacking both tourists and the Marxist government troops, the bus was given a military escort. The guerillas opened fire and the two travellers, Canadian Gaeton Dion and Swiss Kurt Marfut, and three soldiers were killed.

Since the Afghani Embassy in London admit that ambushes are 'happening everywhere, all the time' the presence of the Magic Bus in such a dangerous part of the country is hard to account for. The manager of the firm's London office, Dave Rendall, said this week that the bus was off course and should not have been travelling on that particular route. Magic Bus has another office in Istanbul which organises the trips going further East than Turkey, and it appears that a driver attached to this office had decided to take a short cut. Now Magic Bus in London are selling tickets only as far as Istanbul. It may still be possible to travel further but there will obviously be risks.

As to the actual reason for the attack on the bus, the Afghani Embassy suggest that the ambushers were people who had lost their land after the left-wing revolution which redistributed land to the peasants. Ten years ago travel to the East was fraught enough but now with Iran, Pakistan and India all offering either military or visa problems to intrepid souls, it looks as though it is becoming harder still. *(Duncan Campbell)*

Duncan Campbell's report on the Afghan disaster in Time Out #494, October 1979.

The piece confirms that the Magic Bus office in London was no longer selling overland tickets to India.

The 'Magic Bus' office in Istanbul was a completely different company.

Duncan Campbell

Issue 494 of *Time Out* (dated 5-11 October 1979) carried a short piece about the attack titled *'Magic Bus Afghani Ambush'* with the byline Duncan Campbell.

The magazine actually employed two different Scottish journalists named Duncan Campbell in the 1970s - one was from Glasgow, a thorn in the side of MI5 who was prosecuted under the Official Secrets Act and was gay, while the other was from Edinburgh, a crime reporter who travelled to India in 1971, wrote a novel about the Hippie Trail called *The Paradise Trail*, and married the actress Julie Christie. I'd say it was the latter.

Information supplied that wasn't reported elsewhere included the fact that three Afghan soldiers were killed in the ambush, and that the attackers may - according to the Afghan embassy - have been people who had lost their land after the revolution.

The last advertisement for the Magic Bus to India to appear in Time Out, September 1979.

John Blake

After leaving school in 1966 John Blake had started work at the *Hackney Gazette*, and later founded his *'Ad Lib'* column, a pop culture guide that migrated from the *Evening News* to the *Evening Standard* when the former title folded.

Blake gave several gratuitous plugs to the Magic Bus company over the years, but quite why he was shilling for Greg Williams so enthusiastically is not known. There may have been a personal connection somewhere.

On 5 October 1979, under the heading *"Hippy bus-stop"*, he noted that Magic Bus had stopped running its buses to India, and that while some of the other overland companies were continuing they were all bypassing Afghanistan.

"But none are as cheap as Magic Bus, which started the trips in hippie days", he adds, comparing the company's prices favourably with those of Budget Bus and Top Deck Travel.

The Hostages

On 4 November 1979 the US Embassy in Teheran was stormed by a mob and many hostages were taken. It was a major news story, and anyone thinking of travelling overland to India would have had to take it on board.

Overland operators were accustomed to changing routes to avoid danger zones, but it was not possible to bypass Iran - driving through Soviet Central Asia was simply not an option.

The alternative of air travel was now affordable and the Overland was becoming a niche interest. A few bus operators tried to keep going but there were few takers.

The 'Magic Bus to India' era was coming to an end.

The Last Bus

According to the Canadian author Rory MacLean the 'Magic Bus to India' was terminated by Iran's Ayatollah Khomeini in 1980 when *"the last Magic Bus was hurried out of town by an adolescent guardsman waving his Kalashnikov"*.

Having read his book I would say that if Rory MacLean told me the sky was blue I would go outside to check. And a contemporary press report says that the Magic Bus office in London had stopped selling tickets to India after September 1979:

"Magic Bus have stopped selling overland tickets to India following the murder of two of their passengers in Afghanistan", wrote John Blake in the *Evening News* on 5 October. *"Now the bus company - which used to sell London to Delhi tickets for £97 - will go no further than Istanbul"*.

Later UK press reports confirmed that the service had stopped but blamed the situation in Iran, where the US Embassy had been ransacked in November 1979 - many hostages were taken, and an attempt to rescue them in April 1980 ended in disaster. Then Saddam Hussein started a war with his Iranian neighbours.

The End of the Road

A few bus companies tried to continue, but passengers were scarce and visas were not being issued for US or British passport holders. Some overland buses went through with an armed Iranian guard on board but others had to drive through empty, with passengers flying over. Budget Bus advertised until August 1980 (but may have stopped earlier), Sundowners did flyovers until January 1981 and Top Deck, who also did some flyovers, persisted the longest.

All of which is well documented. And Torkild Bangsbo Andersen told me that on the last successful trip from Copenhagen *"Gerard Wantenaar (aka Dutch Gerard, aka The Flying Dutchman) was the driver"*, that he was required to have an Iranian guard on board, and that some passengers flew over due to the visa issues.

"They chose to take a bus from Ankara to Damascus where I met them and we flew to Karachi, took the train to Quetta and met Gerard and the bus there". He said nothing about the bus being *"hurried out of town by an adolescent guardsman waving his Kalashnikov"*, but then Torkild is not a writer of fiction. He said it was 1979.

UK press reports indicated that it was not possible to buy a bus ticket to India from Magic Bus in London after September 1979, but Fleet Street was notoriously unreliable, while the Amsterdam and Copenhagen offices largely operated autonomously.

Maarten Bolluijt, who was manager of the Magic Bus Amsterdam office at the time, told me about a bus that left for Kathmandu with a Japanese film crew on board - apparently the footage had been shown in Japan in two parts and was very long. Maarten said he had watched it himself at the Rokin office when he worked there in 1982, and very much enjoyed it.

Maarten was involved in getting proper licences for the bus, which started from England. The film had *"beautiful shots of the bus going over the London Bridge"* (he may have meant Tower Bridge). Sadly, I couldn't find a copy to ascertain the exact date.

66 Shaftesbury Avenue, London W.1.
01 439 8471 · Telex 21194

Chapter 5
THE EXPANSION

Main Offices in: London·Amsterdam·Paris·Athens

Amsterdam Office Watch

According to Graham Bourne's book the first Amsterdam office was opened to the public in summer 1974 at Rokin 24 - it was in a building that was already home to the 'Circus' company and other travel businesses.

The second office followed in 1975, located above a Wimpy bar at Damrak 87. Peter Hoornweg was hired as manager (later replaced by Maarten Bolluijt). It was still active in December 1979.

At some point the office moved to Rokin 38 and had step-free access - there are photographs showing a ground floor window with the classic logo signwritten on it, including a shot of the staff (or at least some of them) assembled outside.

Maarten Bolluijt told me that the 'shop' was on the ground floor, the office area was on the first floor, and the third and fourth floors were reserved for living accommodation - Greg Williams apparently stayed there after giving up the flat in Nieuwendijk.

When major riots erupted on 30 April 1980 - the day that Princess Beatrix replaced Queen Juliana - some of the clashes took place on Rokin and many businesses had their windows smashed. But the young rioters didn't target Magic Bus, Maarten recalled.

An additional Magic Bus outlet was then opened at Rokin 10 as *"the new flight office"*. The company was expanding fast.

One photograph in Greg Williams' archive that baffled me shows a ground-floor office in what looks like a side street with many posters in the window written in Dutch and the 'classic' Magic Bus logo prominently displayed.

Maarten identified it as being in Den Haag, and there may have been an office in Rotterdam too - a 1982 article in *Het Vriege Volk* said the company had *"four offices in the major cities"*.

Maarten Bolluijt

Peter Hoornweg had been the first office manager at Damrak 87 in Amsterdam but fell out with Greg Williams and was replaced by Maarten Bolluijt.

Maarten was five years older than Greg and had experience in the travel business - he had actually been involved with the 'Circus' company at Rokin 24, which he described as *"a conglomerate of travel agencies in the same building"*.

He was originally hired to handle the flight department for three weeks, but it soon became apparent that he knew more about the bus industry than anyone else and was put in charge.

When I spoke to Maarten in 2025 he had recently celebrated his 80th birthday but was still sharp as a tack, was very generous with his time, and was extremely helpful.

He dismissed Tony Wheeler's ridiculous claim that the Magic Bus company didn't actually exist, pointing out that *"we transported hundreds of thousands of people"*.

As for Rory MacLean's claim that *"The original Magic Bus operated from a cockroach-infested office on Amsterdam's Dam Square"*, he quickly debunked that myth too - there was never a Magic Bus office there, though it was home to the student travel organisation, described by Graham Bourne as *"a small office tucked away under the rafters above the tottering Mensa building"* and run by *"a gaunt, hairy, bespectacled Dutchman about thirty, named Simon"*.

Maarten Bolluijt told me frankly that when he started with Magic Bus *"everything was done illegally"* - he knew that licences were required, and worked to put things on a legitimate basis. Despite being fired in 1982 he has fond memories of the company.

"I'm very glad that I was part of it", he says.

*Magic Bus Amsterdam staff outside Rokin 38.
Office manager Maarten Bolluijt is on the right.*

The Magic Bus office in Den Haag.

The Magic Bus office at Rokin 38 in Amsterdam. The shop was on the ground floor with the office on the first floor and living quarters on the third and fourth floors.

Rodda Thomas

Originally a passenger on a Magic Bus from Athens, Rodda Thomas took over as courier at the Yugoslav border when the incumbent was found to be drunk and incapable.

Rodda did eight return trips on the Amsterdam-Athens run in total - which he described as fun but exhausting - then found himself working at the Damrak 87 office selling tickets, and later went on to work at Rokin 38 too.

The office on Damrak was above a Wimpy bar, with bus sales on the first floor, plane sales on the second and clerical offices on the third. Rodda never ate a Wimpy himself, but the Egg Cream café was as popular with office staff as it was with bus drivers.

Greg Williams was often out of town and Nee ran the office in a friendly fashion - she told me she remembered Rodda fondly, and I found him a lot of fun when we met up for lunch.

Rodda lived above the shop when he worked at the Rokin 38 office - he said that during the 1980 'coronation riots' he was allowed time off to join the protests - and after the company collapsed he continued to live in Amsterdam for over twenty years.

He certainly seems to have enjoyed his time with Magic Bus, and told me that he socialised with colleagues regularly - names he remembered were Koos, Wim, Sylvia, Hanneke and David (a hairdresser who put his talents to good use for the staff).

The Magic Bus office at Rokin 38 was situated next door to the office of the Israeli airline El Al, and one morning Rodda and other staff awoke to an eerie silence - no trams, no traffic noise - and looking out they saw the building surrounded by straw bales.

It was a bomb scare, but fortunately a false alarm, and after an hour or two everything was back to normal. Phew!

Magic Inn

On 14 January 1980 there was another gratuitous plug for Magic Bus in John Blake's *Ad Lib* column, this time promoting the new Magic Inn. Located near Amsterdam's main station at Nieuwzijds Voorburgwal 27 and said to be run by Steve and Terry, the setup was dormitory accommodation at five beds to a room.

John Blake tells us that *"you can stay in the first Magic Inn for a very reasonable £4.50 bed and breakfast"*, and that you can get there on an overnight bus from Victoria Coach Station for a tenner. There was also a café, bar and disco, he says.

Blake popped up again on 9 September 1980 to plug a Jimi Hendrix memorial festival that was about to be held in Amsterdam. *"And the cheapest way to get to Amsterdam is via Magic Bus, who charge £12 each way"*. Sho' nuff.

Ray Gosling

In July 1980 BBC Radio 4 began broadcasting a series of ten talks by Ray Gosling under the title *On the Train to New Zealand*.

Episode two was *The Magic Bus from the Pudding Shop to Iran* - Gosling had set out in 1979 and had originally planned to use the famous train that was carried by ferry across Lake Van to hook up with the Iranian railway system, but it was not to be.

"With the overthrow of the Shah came the end of the Vangolu Express. No more trains from the West, but the English buses still rumbled through: clapped out old Bedfords with names like Moonshine and The Slug and a picnic of long haired European youths ... but in every squalid Turkish town, as the bus puts up for the night, comes a new question: And what do you think of Khomeini then?"

So the blurb says, but the programme was unavailable - whether an actual Magic Bus was involved has not been confirmed.

The Luchtbus

Before Greg Williams founded his company the Amsterdamse Mobiel Straet Circus Company de Magic Bus ran summer tours of Amsterdam in 1971. On 1 July 1972 it featured in the Dutch paper *NRC Handelsblad* under the headline *"Magic Bus is back"*.

The group was based at Rokin 24 and Greg Williams got to know them well - in 1974 he set up his first office at the same address and had their agreement to trade under the Magic Bus name.

The Circus Company bus was a 1953 Leyland Royal Tiger that was decorated with various motifs, and the tours included visits to counterculture centres. In 1973 it was donated to the Amsterdam Balloon Company (Amsterdams Ballon Gezelschap), a group of artists, poets, actors, clowns and musicians had who squatted in Ruigoord, declared a 'free zone' and artist community.

In winter 1975 the Balloon Company troupe set off for Morocco with 26 people on the bus, now renamed the Luchtbus (Airbus). Two years later they headed for China with the 9-year-old Daniel Boissevain (later a famous actor) on board.

The closest they got was the Nepal-China border in 1980, but it was still an impressive feat. On later trips the group visited Moscow (where they camped in Gorky Park) and East Berlin, and the bus also travelled to England, where it was photographed.

Sadly, the bus was destroyed by a fire at the group's workshop in Ruigoord on 27 December 2022. At least I think it was, as many of the reports that I have read about the Luchtbus are contradictory and the account given above may not be entirely accurate.

One report in *Het Parool* claimed that the bus had been donated by *"the owner of the Magic Bus, the travel organisation that transported young backpackers on the infamous Hippie Trail via Amsterdam and Istanbul to India"*. I'd say that was just 'magical thinking'.

Couriers

Greg Williams had made the decision early on to stop owning any buses and employing drivers - everything was contracted out, and over time the Athens run became dominated by Greek drivers.

They weren't necessarily good with languages, and the solution was to leave them to do the driving and have a Magic Bus courier on board to deal with the passengers.

Graham Bourne doesn't mention couriers, and there are no details in the archive. Most information comes from couriers themselves posting on web forums in the 21st century. Some appear to have seen their job as conducting a three-day party. Yay!

The Courier's Tale

In March 1980 three young friends travelled on a Magic Bus to Athens from London, intending to stay a couple of weeks. One of them was Nigel Howell.

"One month later, with my friends having gone home and after a few beers in the Plaka the night before, I popped into the Magic Bus office to ask if they needed a courier. I was told to come back at two o'clock to take the bus to Munich".

"So off I went, clueless. I was just there to inform the passengers of what lay ahead and to collect passports and payments for visas at the borders. You soon learn when there's no-one to ask".

"In Munich I met the courier from the London bus, a guy from Newcastle-under-Lyme, and we swapped passengers. I took his lot to Athens, he took my lot to London".

Munich was an overnight stop. Nigel partied late, got a brief sleep on the bus, grabbed a bratwurst and coffee breakfast, then headed for Athens *"with a sore head"*.

"In Athens I'd take the passengers to the Peta Inn, opposite the Hotel California. I stayed in the basement free for six months. Geórgios was the owner and Takis (a great guy) was the manager".

"It soon felt like I was part of the Athens scene, lots of friends, good social life and good relations with the shop owners, where I bought groceries, bread, and (of course) gyros. It was great to arrive back from Munich, wake up in the heat, walk to the Plaka and chat with the local traders. It felt like a true community".

"The hostel was a buzzy place, great people, especially when one got a guitar out and just played away with us all singing. And the shower room was interesting too: three shower heads, no doors, and mixed - with a mirror on the opposite wall! How times change".

There were many incidents on the road. Nigel recalled a guy with two passports (British and Israeli) being kicked off the bus by Yugoslav officials, and being kicked off a bus in Yugoslavia himself by the Greek drivers (for reasons untranslated).

He was soon picked up by another Magic Bus, driven by someone he knew, and eventually made his way back to Athens. He worked the route for the full season, and enjoyed himself.

"As well as staying for free at the Peta Inn hostel, I also ate free at a bar-restaurant round the corner, as I used to take passengers there on their first night. So all in all, Athens was cheap for me, hence my £60 weekly cash from Magic Bus never really got spent".

"What a life!"

"I was lucky to meet people from all over the world through travelling and working on the Magic Bus; people from Colombia to France, from Holland to Australia".

"It was the days of free living, cool vibes, no animosity. Would love to turn the clock back and relive it. Great memories".

The Quakes

On the night of 24 February 1981 the Gulf of Corinth was struck by two earthquakes in quick succession, with another hitting the area eleven days later.

At least twenty people died, more than seven thousand buildings were destroyed (over a thousand in Athens), and there was a lot of damage to people and property.

It seems, though, that the Magic Bus office in Athens stayed open throughout, at least if an amusing photograph posted on the web is anything to go by.

"Even eartquakes [sic] don't close Magic Bus", we are told, by what appear to be a couple of workers at the Athens office.

The spelling mistake merely adds to the authenticity, but so far I have been unable to positively identify either of the guys holding up the hastily improvised sign. D'arcy and Dick, perhaps?

Washington Post

On 19 April 1981 the *Washington Post* ran a puff piece by Jane Morse titled *'Finding Your Way In the Bargain Bazaar'*. It explained to its American readers how to get good deals when travelling around Europe and elsewhere. But that's not all.

"'Somewhere else' in the late '60s was India. So Greg Williams, a Briton, bought himself an old bus and recruited a load of like-minded passengers who also wanted to head east. But first he applied some paint and turned the bus into a spectacle that struck some observers dumb. One stayed calm enough to say, "That's magic!" and thus a great name was born".

How many origin stories does that make now?

"Slowly but surely, Williams built a company to go with the name and began 'scheduled' service between Europe and the subcontinent. It was of course, the flaky way to go. On one trip a driver reportedly fell in love with one of the passengers and refunded everyone else's ticket cost so he could terminate the trip and attend to private business".

Citation needed? It may well be true, but who reported it?

"On another occasion, according to a still-satisfied customer's story, the bus's windshield was blown out as passengers and crew tooled through the Alps, but they plunged on to Athens before having it fixed".

"At some borders, authorities - not without reason - have suspected dopers were aboard and brought dogs around for a sniff or ripped up a seat or two. But not even the Magic Bus had enough magic to keep going to India after Iran blew up. The events in Afghanistan merely added a final fillip".

It's all nonsense, but that last sentence is just disgusting.

The people who died deserved better.

London Office Watch

The first Magic Bus 'office' in London was a domestic property in Richmond in March 1974, moving by July to 27 Giesbach Road near Archway. The operation then moved to actual office premises at 637 Holloway Road nearby in January 1975.

A central London office followed at 74 Shaftesbury Avenue later that year and in September 1977 it moved just a few doors down to number 66 Shaftesbury Avenue.

Barrie Moreton told me that Greg Williams had later said he was having *"serious problems"* with the London office and asked him to intervene and train the new manager, Dave Rendall. Barrie did six months, starting on 1 December 1979.

Magic Bus moved to 67-69 New Oxford Street in July 1981. My understanding is that this is the office in a lot of the archive photographs, with the large murals featuring a train and a seaplane amongst other delights.

Studying the images, what I find interesting - apart from the people - is the ephemera on display. There are signs, brochures, leaflets, and some t-shirts too, though sadly nothing is in close up. There is a shot of a sign outside that is definitely from New Oxford Street - one of the buildings in the background is still standing and easily identified. The shop was apparently on the ground floor.

One web post said Magic Bus had *"a large office in Percy Street"* (and another claimed one in New Bond Street) but I couldn't find any other references to either. Successor companies perhaps?

Testimony from the staff who worked at the London offices is rare - the archive had photographs but no names. The closest I got was a guy who had loaded passengers at St Pancras in the 1980s - what became the site of the British Library was used for bus departures, and I remember dropping off a friend there myself.

Marisa Explains It All

My luck changed when I was introduced to Marisa, who had worked at the 66 Shaftesbury Avenue office in 1979-80.

Marisa told me that a friend who loaded passengers at St Pancras - and who sometimes had to give the drivers a bung when the seats were overbooked - had alerted her about a job in ticket sales.

The work could be demanding - during peak season there would be customers queuing outside before the office opened, as by this time Magic Bus had become a major success.

On the other hand, the wages were good compared to other firms and it was *"a really fun place to work"*, Marisa told me.

David Rendall was the general manager, Nick Weston ran Magic Plane, with Wendy Fellowes, Valerie Haynes, Dierdre, Paulette and Linda also working in the office at the time.

Marisa said that she met Greg Williams twice (once in London and once in Amsterdam) and described him as *"a perfect gentleman"*. She recalled being at work when news of the Afghanistan disaster came in - passengers being shot dead had a sobering effect.

There was also an attempted robbery of the Magic Plane department, when an armed man was reported in the building and a police lockdown ensued. Scary stuff, but Marisa's memories were mostly positive, and she enjoyed working for the company.

Marisa identified some of the staff in the photographs but had moved on before the business relocated to New Oxford Street (where her sister worked in the accounts department). The shop was said to be so busy that a paid entertainer was provided for those waiting in the queue.

Never a dull moment with Magic Bus.

Some of the staff at the New Oxford Street office.

Nick Weston

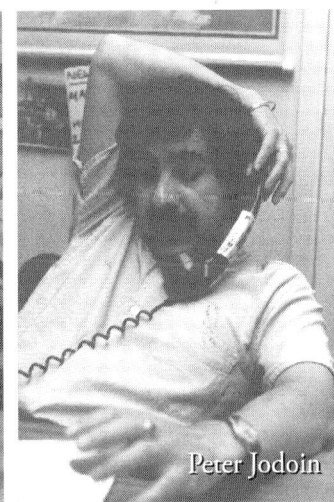
Peter Jodoin

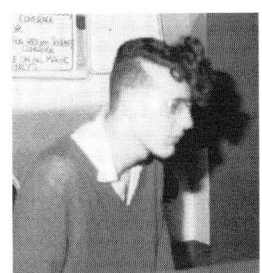

Magic Bus office in New Oxford Street.

New Oxford Street staff looking busy for the camera.
Opposite: T-shirts on sale in New Oxford Street.

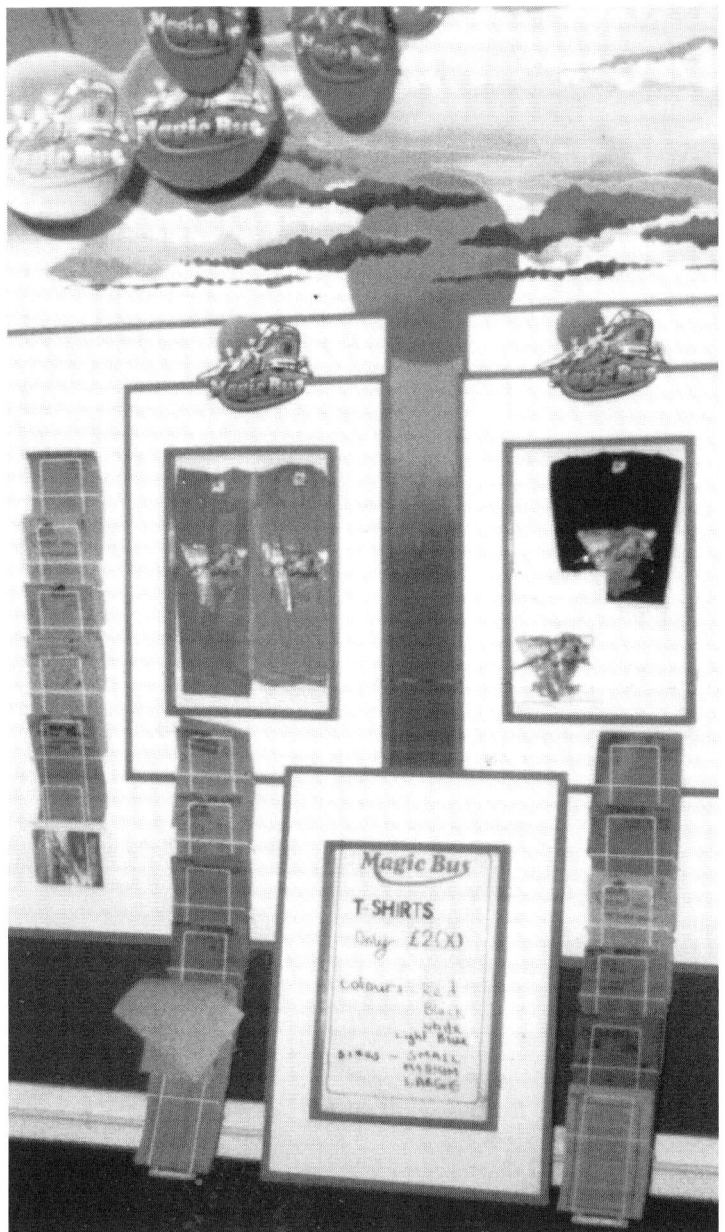

ATHENS EXPRESS

ITMA

On 10 November 1981 it was that man John Blake again, but this time his *Ad Lib* column was in the *Evening Standard* and he was the bearer of tragic news: *"End of the line for Magic Bus"*.

But it was just Pete Townshend's Richmond bookshop.

Antwerp

Documents in the archive from August 1981 show an *'Application for registration by a natural person'* in Dutch. My understanding is that what we knew then as the 'Benelux' countries - Belgium, Holland and Luxembourg - pooled such matters.

Greg gives his business address as Rokin 38 under the company name 'International Pullman', but the application is from Antwerp at Bisschoppenhoflaan 284 - Maarten Bolluijt suggested that this may have been his accountant's address.

Don't Believe The Hype

A trawl of the newspaper archives reveals that in the 1980s Magic Bus was busy expanding its UK office network, with agency deals in place in Manchester, Liverpool and Aberdeen.

A puff piece in *The Guardian* on 13 March 1982 stated that *"Magic Bus has anything up to 60 coaches on the road on any one day, going all over Europe"* - suggesting vehicle ownership - and that *"Last year, half a million people travelled with them"* (which may be true). But *"Travel to India has been suspended due to difficulties in Iran"*.

It had actually stopped in 1979 when two passengers were shot dead in Afghanistan, but you wouldn't want to mention *that* in a sales promotion. Magic Train gets a plug, and so does 'Magic Circle', *"which offers a round trip London-Paris-Amsterdam-London for only £29"* as part of a *"broader spectrum"* of options.

Diversions

As Magic Bus became successful it attracted increasing attention from the authorities - there were strict rules and regulations, and the company was flagrantly non-compliant.

For buses from London the main problem was the East Kent Bus Company monopoly on services to Dover. Greg Williams also complained in his 1972 interview with *Peninsular West* about the regulations in the 'Common Market' countries.

But for any regulations to be effective they require enforcement, for which resources seems to have been distinctly lacking, with the few officials involved expecting branded services that used regular routes and schedules. Magic Bus services on the continent, though, had the flexibility to use the less popular border crossings at times when the officials were unlikely to be active.

As the authorities wised up and got their act together the direct route to Athens *via* Cologne and Frankfurt became more problematic, with buses increasingly going *via* Strasbourg and Stuttgart, or further south through Paris, Lyon, Milan and Venice, a route that allowed Z-plate vehicles to avoid Germany all summer.

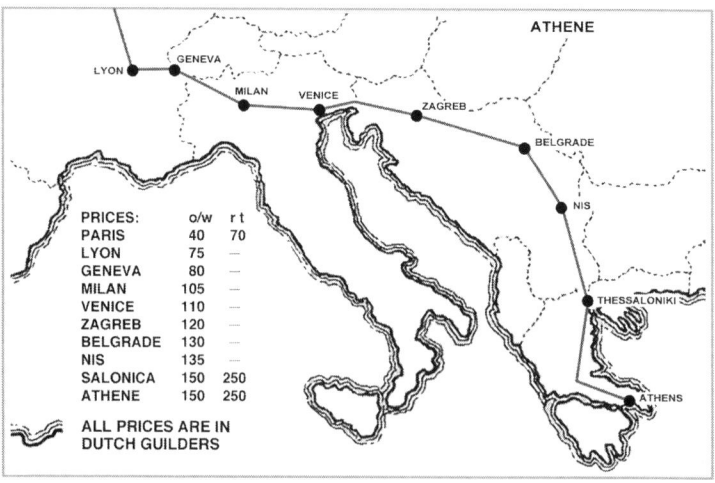

Geneva

While Geneva was listed as a destination on the southern route, the buses didn't actually enter Switzerland - they stopped instead at the French town of Saint-Julien-en-Genevois, located right on the border, just five miles from the city centre.

Some earlier buses had used the Mont Blanc tunnel, but that was at the discretion of the independent contractors, who could choose to use the tunnel and pay the toll if it suited them - it was a trade-off with the extra time and fuel costs.

Yugoslavia

The country named Yugoslavia existed between 1918 and 1992, comprising the modern states of Slovenia, Croatia, Serbia, Bosnia & Herzegovina, Montenegro, Kosovo and North Macedonia.

In the Magic Bus era it was a non-aligned communist federation, though never part of the Eastern Bloc - most westerners could transit the country without a visa, and Yugoslav passport holders could travel freely in most of Europe during the Cold War.

Yugoslavia had its attractions, but for most of us travelling overland to Athens, Istanbul, Kabul or Kathmandu in those days it was not a place we wanted to stop in, just one that couldn't be avoided.

The roads were poor, the language was incomprehensible, and few remember having fun there - though to be fair to the locals, most of us treated it as an obstacle to get through as fast as possible, travelling the Brotherhood and Unity Highway through Zagreb, Belgrade, Niš and Skopje (or *vice versa*).

In later years Magic Bus planned holiday trips along the Dalmatian coast to Dubrovnik, and I've heard that a successor company even visited Albania, but in 1992 the outbreak of civil war in the Balkans finished off Yugoslavia as a nation state.

Brindisi

One way to bypass Yugoslavia without travelling through any of the Iron Curtain countries was to use the ferry from Brindisi in southern Italy to a port in southern Greece.

One popular option was Patras - it took more than twenty hours and it wasn't for landlubbers, but some people enjoy life afloat and if you were heading for the Greek Islands you were going to be using ferries anyway. Piraeus was another option.

On these routes Dutch buses (often Bovo Tours) were generally used in Holland, Belgium and France, Italian buses were used in Italy and Greek buses were used in Greece.

Cosa Nostra

A 1994 article in *The Independent* newspaper- about which more later - had London office manager David Rendall recounting a tale about an incident in Italy in the early 1980s. It was a very brief reference, told from a London viewpoint, and gave little detail.

One of my correspondents (who prefers anonymity) was actually there. He and his girlfriend, both of whom worked for Magic Bus, were on their way back from Athens *via* Brindisi, where an Italian coach was waiting. It would take Magic Bus passengers as far as Lake Como, where they would transfer to a Dutch bus - but the deal required payment in cash, which had not been made.

The Magic Bus passengers were driven into the hills and kept at a youth hostel for three days until the money arrived - but my correspondent and his Italian girlfriend were put up in a luxury hotel, taken out to restaurants, and treated as honoured guests.

Over dinner it was explained to them that Greg Williams needed to make his cash payments on time, and they were shown a Beretta pistol to make the message to him clear. *Capisce?*

*A photograph from Greg Williams' archive
that has been preserved for posterity.
The date and location are unknown
- and so is the reason for the request.*

California Dreaming

The Jane Morse article in the *Washington Post* on 19 April 1981 was very much a 'puff piece' aimed at an American audience, and it included this revealing paragraph:

"The Magic Bus now proudly contracts for "brand-new, modern buses, properly registered and insured", says Ramon Rebel, who runs the company's U.S. ticket office -- selling seats at slightly higher than London prices -- in Van Nuys, Calif... And with the shorter trips, he says, they're also attracting "quite a few" over-30s and bargain-hunting nondopers".

Van Nuys is a district of Los Angeles and Ramon Rebel was the proprietor of Rebel Tours - the office was his, and the *"slightly higher than London prices"* would represent his commission.

That Ramon Rebel stresses the *"brand-new, modern buses, properly registered and insured"* as something new reflects the fact that these elements had previously been lacking.

Maarten Bolluijt told me that he had been involved in setting up the Magic Bus presence in California as he already knew the people there, who he described as friends.

Apparently he flew out personally to make the arrangements with Rebel Tours - in addition to the Los Angeles office there was one planned for San Francisco.

Maarten also told me that the Magic Bus San Francisco office was on Clement Street, just north of Golden Gate Park. A photograph from Greg's archive shows Michael Willemsen playing peek-a-boo for the camera at the temporary premises, *"a rented cabin on the street"* in front of the office itself, which I had originally assumed had been taken in Holland or Denmark.

Maarten said that the actual shop never opened.

The temporary Magic Bus office in San Francisco.

The Magic of Magic Bus

On 9 April 1982 a syndicated puff piece in some of the Irish papers gave a Magic Bus office address at St Andrew Street in Dublin. The article was titled *'The Magic of Magic Bus'*.

"Magic Bus was founded rather unceremoniously", the piece begins, *"by a young Englishman named Greg Williams, whom in seeking adventure in the late 1960's organised the purchase of an old bus with the intentions of driving it with some friends to India. Being successful with the first trip a second journey by bus was soon planned and similarly successfully executed"*.

Yet another origin myth.

"By the fall of 1978 approximately four hundred passengers a week were being booked by bus from Europe to India. It was at that time estimated that the total bus passengers to India carried by Magic Bus would exceed ten thousand during the calendar year of 1979".

"Unfortunately however political turmoil struck Iran in the latter part of 1978 forcing Magic Bus to curtail its overland traffic to India and necessarily involving the refunding and cancellations of a considerable number of tickets".

Shameless. A Magic Bus trip to India had been crossing Afghanistan in September 1979 when it was attacked and two passengers were shot dead. No passengers were refunded.

We are then told that Magic Plane had sold over 1,250 tickets to India already that year and that the company employed *"73 people in 14 branch or representative offices throughout Western Europe"*, with two new offices in Dublin and Barcelona due to open later that month. Business was clearly brisk.

We hear at the end of the article that *"Offices have now been opened in San Francisco and Los Angeles"* - it seems clear that the company was expanding rapidly.

Greg Williams, travel agent.

Magic Ski

The *Belfast Telegraph* of 10 December 1982 carried an unusual ad for 'Magic Ski' using a variation of the classic logo.

"For full colour brochure contact Magic Bus", the ad says, giving the address as *"Angier Street, Dublin"* with alternative options *via* student services at two universities in Northern Ireland.

After that it was downhill all the way.

66 Shaftesbury Avenue, London W.1.
01 439 8471 · Telex 21194

Chapter 6
THE IMPLOSION

Main Offices in: London·Amsterdam·Paris·Athens

The Collapse

The Magic Bus Travel Company collapsed on Xmas Eve 1982.

The first press report I could find was published in the *Daily Mirror* on Monday 27 December, which said that another company had initially *"promised to honour the Magic Bus tickets"*. Yay!

"But the company, Top Deck Travel, asked for extra payments and some clients paid an extra £50 to continue their Christmas holidays". Possibly a case of 'Skroo you, Greg Williams'.

The next day brought articles galore. The *Belfast Telegraph* noted that *"The collapse of the Dublin-based Magic Bus travel service has hit a number of Ulster people wanting to spend the New Year in Paris"*. Some ticket-holders were allowed to cross the Irish Sea on the Holyhead-Dun Laoghaire ferry without paying twice.

The *Birmingham Mail* reported that tickets issued by National Express were also being honoured to some extent, and a travel agent in Derby had managed to transfer most bookings but was surprised at the turn of events at Magic Bus - *"We even received a Christmas card from them"*, the company's manager told the man from the *Derby Evening Telegraph*.

The *Edinburgh Evening News* and many other papers reported that passengers wanting refunds would have to wait until after a creditors meeting on 21 January. The *Hartlepool Mail* and Wolverhampton's *Express & Star* noted that Grey Green Coaches had offered to take passengers for *"three-quarters of our normal price"* - this was also reported in the *Daily Mirror*, but the reporter from *The Guardian* had the most detailed coverage:

"The Magic Bus has ground to a halt", wrote Nick Davies. *"After nearly 20 years on a shoe string, the company which beat the Russians in Afghanistan and the Ayatollah in Iran has finally fallen foul of an old-fashioned capitalist cash crisis"*. Seriously?

Magic Bus company goes bust

Magic Bus passengers must wait for refund

Magic Bus cash is delayed.

PASSENGERS booked on the cheap long-distance coach firm Magic Bus, which collapsed on Christmas Eve, will have to wait until after a creditors' meeting on January 21 for any refunds, a company spokesman said yesterday.

Other coach companies, specialising in trips to Dublin, Amsterdam, Paris, Frankfurt and Cologne, offered discount fares to passengers stranded when Magic Bus ceased trading.

"We will take Magic Bus passengers for three-quarters of our normal price," said John Card, traffic manager of one of the rescue firms, Grey-Green Coaches.

Crash of coach firm surprise to booking agents

STAFF at a Derby travel agents were called off their holiday to help sort out the problems caused by the collapse of the Magic Bus travel firm.

Travel firm 'in a mess'

The Guardian Myth

It's bizarre. The Magic Bus company had lasted ten years and the idea that it 'beat' the Russians is just insane. But there's more:

"The company started in the Sixties by Greg Williams, who was wandering around India in the approved fashion. He decided to run a mini-bus - brightly painted with gold seats - from Delhi to Kabul and charge his passengers £5 a head".

"The routes to the East were blocked by revolution in Iran and then by invasion in Afghanistan", Nick Davies tells us, *"but the Magic Bus found a way through".*

Nothing in those paragraphs is true. Nick Davies was a young reporter back then, starting out in 1976 and joining *The Guardian* in July 1979. He later had a stellar career, seen on ITV's *World In Action* and going on to expose the *News of the World* phone-hacking scandal. But his copy above is just embarrassing.

"Magic Bus was registered recently as a limited liability company, but it was short of capital to finance its expansion. For the last three months, staff have known that a crisis was imminent".

Now that looks like real journalism - registering for limited liability just before going bust would seem decidedly dodgy. Sadly I was unable to find a copy of the company registration.

"In an effort to save the company it was arranged to sell the title to a consortium of Belgians in the second week of January", we hear. *"But on December 23, Mr Williams and his manager, David Rendall, realised they did not have the cash to pay for the coaches which they had chartered for Christmas travellers".*

"They arranged for passengers to be transferred to Euroways and Grey Green Coaches, and left a brief message on their answering machine apologising for the disruption. 'Finally we wish you a Happy New Year', it said. 'Goodbye'".

Het Vrige Volk, 27 December 1982

Dutch Coverage

There were also Dutch press reports about the Magic Bus collapse on 27 December 1982 - one was in *NRC Handelsblad* with the title *"Magic Bus zit aan de grond"* (which an online translator rendered as *"Magic Bus sits on the ground"*) though the rest of the text in the copy I saw was illegible. Another appeared in *Het Vriege Volk*.

"Magic Bus has to cancel 1500 bus passengers" said the headline under the standfirst *"Branch of British company in trouble"*.

The company had *"stopped all trips with immediate effect, due to financial difficulties"*, the article said, adding that *"The twenty people who work at Magic Bus Nederland will be dismissed"*.

"The travel agency has four offices in the major cities. The spokesman of Magic Bus in Amsterdam says that the problems have arisen at the central organization in London".

I know of two Amsterdam offices and one in the Hague - I would guess that the fourth was in Rotterdam. The piece said that some ticket-holders were transferred to Bovo-Tours of Roelofarendseen and that the service to London that day went ahead with 240 passengers carried across the English Channel.

The Rescue

The *Daily Mirror* on 6 January 1983 gave details of a newly-formed 'Magic Bus Passengers Group' that hoped to assist with refunds in the aftermath. On 14 January the *Marylebone Mercury* gave details of the creditors meeting, to be held in the New Oxford Street office on 21 January at 11 o'clock.

On 22 January 1983 *The Guardian* reported that the company had been rescued by a consortium which was taking over *"the old Magic Bus offices"* at 67-69 New Oxford Street from the owners, who (it was later said) had actually taken over from Greg Williams in November the previous year.

The new owners were not named, but *"the new company would be called the Magic Bus Travel Co 1983"*, it was revealed. *"The new company has finances available to meet all the liabilities of Magic Bus Ltd"*, said Christopher Ward of accountants Temple Gothard. *"We will offer refunds or replacement tickets"*.

How many passengers ever got a pay out is not recorded. But the Magic Bus company would *"start trading again within two weeks"*, the piece said, and there is some evidence that it did - though I was unable to find any advertisements.

Déjà Vu

A travel section puff piece in *The Guardian* on 9 July 1983 told us that *"the resilient Magic Bus operation will shuttle you to Munich and back for £54 - likely as not alongside passengers paying full fare. It is not commonly known that Magic Bus merely lease seats on other company's vehicles. The trade are happy to swop [sic] discounted tickets for the marketing allure of the Magic Bus name"*.

But two weeks later the new company also went bust, unable to meet its commitments to the liquidator of the previous mess. The Magic Bus company had debts of £98,994 when it was wound up, *The Guardian* revealed.

Liquidation

On 23 July 1983 *The Guardian* reported on the previous day's creditors meeting, which heard that a Tony Carter, who had fronted the rescue plan, had not come up with the promised funds, *"and less than £2,000 was paid to people who had bought useless tickets"*.

Tony Carter, man of mystery - I have not seen his name elsewhere, and an earlier piece in *The Guardian* had spoken of a "*consortium of Belgians*" being involved.

But there was more: *"The meeting heard that Mr Carter was acting as a consultant to yet another company, Magic Bus Services, which is trading at the firm's old headquarters"*.

Michael Radford, the original liquidator, was quoted by the paper as saying *"Quite frankly, the whole thing is an awful mess"* - and it would be hard to argue with that.

Barrie Moreton felt that it was *"purely a cash problem, they couldn't pay the bills"* - the company was apparently viable on paper, but had failed to ensure that its own invoices were paid promptly. Whatever the cause, the effect was disaster.

The Missing Link

The *Time Out* archives for 1983 that I consulted were incomplete, but the surviving issues contained no advertisements for the Magic Bus Travel Co (1983) - it may be that the Greg Williams company had owed money when it went bust, but I couldn't find any advertising in other publications either.

In fact, the only promotion that I know of was the puff-piece in *The Guardian* mentioned earlier - and meanwhile the competition was hammering home their advantage, offering cheap fares on the routes previously covered by Magic Bus, which seems to have become effectively invisible.

The Successors

Magic Bus offices in Athens and Istanbul were run independently and continued in business - young Europeans didn't suddenly stop taking summer holidays, and there are many posts on the web from passengers who used the bus services after 1983. Some successor Magic Bus trips reportedly went through Albania.

My colleague Gerard Aartsen turned up a couple of ads from the Dutch press in 1984 offering Magic Bus and Magic Plane services, one of which gave the address as Rokin 38.

> **MAGIC** PLANE retours: London ƒ 340, Wenen ƒ 560, Bombay/Delhi ƒ 1540, Colombo ƒ 1535, Tokyo ƒ 2140, Australië ƒ 2650 and all the rest. Rokin 38 A'dam. Tel. 020-241858. Businfo 020-264434.

> **MAGIC** BUS/PLANE. Lid Gar. Fonds. Alle **bus-** en (verre) vluchtenbestemmingen tegen de laagste prijzen. Pendelbussen naar de wintersport ƒ 135 ret. Informatie: Bussen 020-264434 Vluchten 020-264844.

Advertisements in the Dutch press from August/September 1984

I was baffled by this until I spoke to Maarten Bolluijt, who shed some much-needed light on the situation. Maarten had been dismissed by Greg Williams two months before the collapse (and was replaced by the returning Peter Hoornweg). He had predicted that a financial crisis was looming as the company was becoming overstretched, but his views were not welcome and were considered *"negative"*. Cassandra would understand.

He soon found employment with another company, which took over the Rokin 10 office and traded as Budget Bus (unrelated to the English company) then Eurolines - *"the Magic Bus was still at Rokin 38 and we bought it a year later"*, he said.

Under this company the Magic Bus name did appear on some of the buses - *"it was a trademark and it was all legal"*, says Maarten - with magnetic stickers used rather than paint or vinyl.

Miracle Bus

The Guardian of 18 April 1987 wrote about Miracle Bus, which it revealed was *"formed by staff from Magic Bus, which long ago ran services for coach-hippy passengers to Asia"*.

The Miracle Bus Company seems to have been founded in 1983, advertising heavily in *Time Out* that year. Which former members of the Magic Bus staff were involved remains a mystery, but they can't be criticised for finding alternative employment and they seem to have been reasonably successful.

Their office was located near Charing Cross at 408 Strand WC2 (close to the Adelphi Theatre), a busy area with plenty of footfall, and they were there for at least five years.

A 1983 advertisement describes them as *"Consolidators for: Grey Green, Euroways, Bovo Tours etc"* and they seemed to have been entirely commission-based, owning no buses themselves. Another reference that I found suggests that the company was promoted on the pirate station Radio Caroline.

"The Miracle Bus people have upset Hoverspeed", the 1987 piece in *The Guardian* said - the company was offering a service using flights from Southend to Ostend that cut two hours from the established hovercraft route, despite using Vickers Viscount turboprop planes that had first been introduced in 1948.

Hoverspeed had lodged a protest with the licensing authority, and it seems they weren't the first. A question in Parliament, which was raised by Southend MP Teddy Taylor and recorded in *Hansard* on 4 May 1988, revealed that Miracle Bus had been trying to set up a similar service since 1985 without success.

Miracle Bus also made the *Washington Post* on 8 October 1988 as *"a London-based bus firm with a different approach"*, but that was the last reference I could find.

PARIS WEEKENDS £38.50 YEAR ROUND

AMSTERDAM*	£15	£28
PARIS	£16	£28.50
MUNICH*	£42	£66
ATHENS	£32	£62
HEIDELBERG	£18.90	£38
SWITZERLAND	£42	£70
STOCKHOLM	£60	£97

*From

ATHENS JET/COACH £79 RETURN

**Discount Worldwide Flights
408 Strand, London WC2.
Bus/Train: 379 6055
Flights: 379 3322**

Consolidators for: Grey Green, Euroways, Bovo Tours etc.

The Miracle Bus Company was reportedly founded by former Magic Bus staff and advertised frequently in Time Out.

Supabus

The *Belfast Telegraph* reported on 18 May 1983 that bus company National Express was forming a new division to sell tickets for European coach routes: *"The services offered by Scottish Bus, Wallace Arnold, Grey Green and Harris coaches... will be incorporated into the selling operation"*, the piece said.

Interestingly, we are told that *"Mr David Rendall, former general manager of Magic Bus, will head the division"* - it would be given the brand name 'Supabus', and under that name it immediately began advertising heavily in *Time Out*. Independently, two sources told me that they had heard the Magic Bus name was sold to Grey-Green for one pound, though it was never used.

Stagecoach

In 1986 Ann Gloag, who came from a family of bus drivers and who co-founded the Stagecoach company with her brother Brian Souter, began a Magic Bus service in Glasgow.

They seem to have acquired the name when coach services were deregulated in 1985. The name was also deployed elsewhere and in 1996 the Stagecoach group introduced their Magic Bus brand to Manchester, where it was used continually until 2025.

Torkild Bangsbo Andersen told me that he had met Brian Souter a few times *"in late 1978 or early 1979"* at the Magic Bus office in Shaftesbury Avenue - Greg Williams' company had actually sold tickets for Souter's student charter buses between Edinburgh and London, before he and his sister founded Stagecoach.

Independent Memories

On 2 August 1994 *The Independent* ran a piece by Simon Calder titled *"Days that the magic died"*, in which the author recalled his experience of travelling with Magic Bus in 1975.

"The idea of spending three and a half days on one of these mobile youth hostels did not sound especially magical, but £27 for 2,000 miles of travel was", Simon tells us. *"That frightful week, I caught the last bus home from Athens. Buying a ticket was reassuringly tricky. You had to find a certain doorway in a side street off Syntagma Square, climb four flights of rickety stairs to a scruffy office where 1,700 drachmas changed hands. Your name was laboriously and inaccurately added to a passenger list and you were handed a scrap of paper which purported to be a ticket".*

Contributors included Minna Daum, who had just left school and hung around in the rain near Victoria Coach Station waiting for the Magic Bus to turn up. *"I'd thought it would be psychedelic, but it was a just an ordinary, boring old coach".*

Ian Lucas sold tickets for successor company Miracle Bus. *"One of the beauties about it was that there was no actual bus. We just hired coaches or bought space on existing services, but people assumed they were getting something special. It was a marketing dream".*

Simon Calder found the journey more of a nightmare. *"A ropey old Bedford 53-seater, hopelessly unsuited to foreign travel"* (which the passengers had to push-start every time it stopped) did not impress him, and he also complained (not unreasonably) that *"Tubular Bells was played continuously for three and a half days".*

"Athens to London was just a very long bus ride", he wrote. *"We left thinking we were pioneers, but arrived merely as passengers, and a pretty miserable bunch at that".* So the article was a mixture of eyewitness experience and research, which also featured quotes from a certain David Rendall.

David Rendall

David Thomas Shuttleworth Rendall, born in May 1952, first got involved with Magic Bus in 1979 - according to Barrie Moreton there had been problems at the London office and Greg Williams had hired him to help out. Barrie's temporary job was to show David Rendall how to run the business efficiently.

David was mentioned in press reports on the company collapse as being the London office manager, and as we have seen was hired in 1983 to run the National Express Supabus brand (he is listed at Companies House as having been a director).

He also held directorships over the years with Monarch Coaches, Flightlink, National Express and Eurolines UK, but I have been unable to trace him for this project and know no more.

His contribution to Simon Calder's 1994 article in *The Independent* was brief but interesting:

"'*At one stage we were operating 25 buses a week down to Athens*', *recalls David Rendall who was general manager for Magic Bus in the late Seventies. Although Magic Bus and its rivals have long since ceased to exist, Mr Rendall still runs a coach to Athens*".

"*His new poacher-turned-gamekeeper role is as managing director for Eurolines (UK). The fare these days, however, is £206 - more than the scheduled flight on Virgin Atlantic. One reason for the increase, he says, is that corners are no longer cut*".

"*At one stage we were using an Italian coach company who would only operate for cash. One night our courier forgot the money, and the boss of the coach firm pulled a gun on him and said 'Tell your boss, next time he comes over here he goes home in a box'*".

As we have seen, there was rather more to this story, but David Rendall wasn't actually there himself.

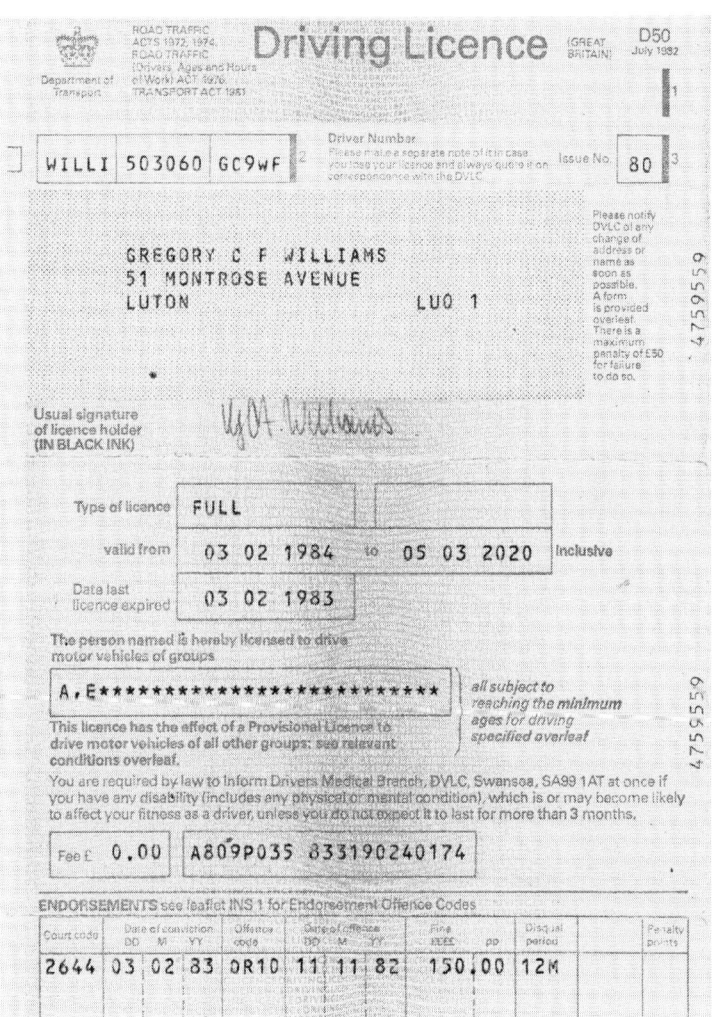

*Offence Code DR10 is an endorsement for
"Driving or attempting to drive with alcohol level above limit".*

*The offence was committed on 11 November 1982.
Greg Williams was fined £150 and banned for a year by
Marlborough Street Magistrates on 3 February 1983.*

66 Shaftesbury Avenue, London W.1.
01 439 8471 · Telex 21194

Chapter 7
THE AFTERMATH

Main Offices in: London·Amsterdam·Paris·Athens

Under The Radar

Greg Williams' archive contains a number of formal documents from November 1983 concerning a flat at Leiebos 29 in Antwerp, which may have been his accountant's address after moving from Bisschoppenhoflaan. On 29 November the last letter says it has been vacated, the keys left with the caretaker, and that a forwarding address would be provided in due course.

Greg was issued with a new UK driving licence on 3 February 1984 having served a one-year ban for drink driving. His address is given on the document as 51 Montrose Avenue, Luton, a comfortable semi-detached property with off-street parking.

I know nothing more about it, and neither did anyone I spoke to. One of life's mysteries, at the time of writing.

For the following couple of years Greg Williams was conspicuously absent. It is possible that disgruntled creditors were a factor but that would only be speculation.

Almost all information from the following period is derived from the documents preserved in Greg Williams' archive, in which the name Jacky comes up frequently.

Jacky

Barrie Moreton described Jacky as *"a very good friend"* of Greg's, and she certainly seems to be someone he trusted.

Some of Greg's letters from the 1980s give Jacky's home address in Upland Road, Dulwich SE22, and in one he specifically says that she would know where to forward replies. A partial diary from 1988 shows that Greg often had dinner with her, but other than that she remains a mystery.

There are worse things to be.

Togo

It seems that in 1986 Greg Williams had driven a Trans-Sahara Express tour to Togo, with a group of hardy westerners in a truck. There are plenty of photographs from the expedition but no written accounts that I know of.

Greg bought a customised Land Rover in Togo and returned to London in it, driving around with Togolese plates.

On 3 August 1986 Greg wrote to Barrie Moreton, then in Niger, about contacts in Togo (who Greg was familiar with) from Jacky's address in Dulwich:

"Enclosed is the print out for the India trips I have started to advertise.. well it comes out this week so as yet I don't know the responce [sic] but I guess it will be allright. As you see I'm offering departures every month so already a cirtain [sic] amount of trips are full, both to India and Togo. I'm now going to start looking for buses trucks or whatever it takes although I've said on both brochures that the trip is run in Mercedes buses. If you meet any serious looking people on the way that could owner/drive any of the trips let them know my address. You are still booked for the Nov. trip but I may try to start in Oct and every month through the winter for both India and Africa and see how it pans out".

The India trips were being organised by Barrie Moreton's Phoenix company, and Greg was doing what he did best, putting bums on seats. The letter finishes with *"It would be good to see if we could start running trips to East Africa"*. But that never happened.

****

In January 2017 someone named Torben posted online to say that he had been a Magic Bus courier and that Greg Williams *"went on to become a truck driver out of Togo, where he also passed away"*. Frankly, it wasn't very helpful.

*Above: The Trans-Sahara Express bound for Togo.
Below: Land Rover driven from Togo to London.*

Phoenix Overland

Barrie Moreton wasn't involved with the Magic Bus company when it collapsed in 1982 - he had left in May 1980 to pursue other interests, including a personal trip to New Zealand and a 20-week tour of South America which he drove for Aardvark in 1981.

After further travels (including visiting Nee in USA) he then led a Trans-Sahara tour for an Oxford University expedition, driving a Peugeot while the group followed in Land Rovers.

At some point Barrie met Greg Williams again in London, and as we have seen Greg drove a tour to Togo himself in 1986, and also began booking tickets for Barrie's new venture.

It is not widely remembered that in the late 1980s and early 1990s it was once again possible to drive overland to India *via* Iran - though Iranian visas were hard to get for British passport holders (and generally unavailable for US citizens).

By this time it was far cheaper to fly if you just wanted to go to India, and 'fast' 20-day bus trips to Delhi made no sense, but there was still a market for the longer cultural tours.

In 1986 Barrie drove a tour to Goa and Kathmandu (where he sold the bus) with Helen and Caroline Straw on board - the sisters had been heading for Australia, but enjoyed the trip so much that the idea of doing it regularly led to the birth of Phoenix Overland.

Once again Greg and Barrie were working together, each doing what they did best - Barrie driving and Greg selling tickets - but Greg's involvement was just a brief stopgap, and he soon moved on to other ventures.

Barrie, Helen and Caroline, on the other hand, kept going as Phoenix Expeditions until retirement in 2008.

*Helen Straw, Greg Williams and Caroline Straw
in front of a Phoenix Overland bus.
Photograph by Barrie Moreton.*

Tenerife

The next letter from Greg to Barrie Moreton is from the Canary Islands on 26 February 1987 and begins with an apology:

"Dear Barrie, Sorry I missed you but I had to get out of England before turning into a vegetable. It seems everything I've tried to do there didn't work out. I must have broken a mirror at some time, and be on a string of bad luck".

Greg had taken a job in Tenerife selling time shares.

"Phil is looking after the trips, though this one doesn't look particularly good, there has been so much news about the Iran/Iraq war and the problems in the Punjab that I guess it's put a lot of people off. We delayed the trip till the 15 March to try to get some more passengers but not too much luck".

Greg ends by telling Barrie to write to him either in Tenerife or (failing that) *"via Jacky who will know where I am".*

The final letter from Greg to Barrie is dated 7 April 1987, and the Upland Road address is given - though Greg explains that he is actually still in Tenerife.

"The timeshare deal went a bit wrong", Greg admits, adding that *"It really is a bit of a rip off working for these companies"*. He didn't even start work - he had never worked for anyone else before and felt that *"the shock would be too much"*.

He says that he is having a good time, likes living there and has even *"given up the booze"*. And he had other plans.

"I'm almost back in the bus business... All being well I'll have two buses doing circular tours of the island... and tomorrow I negotiate for two offices in Puerto".

"Maybe within two weeks Magic Bus will be running again!"

Goa

According to Barrie Moreton - who was unsure of the year - Greg Williams visited Goa one winter, hanging out with Kevin Buckley, Andy Kirk and other members of the old Magic Bus crew.

It would probably have been around Xmas, always peak season, and given other documents in the archive 1988 seems to be the likeliest candidate, but I couldn't get confirmation.

Dear Diary

An appointments diary for 1988 in the archive suggests that Greg started the year selling used cars (as he had done in the 1960s) and that he met with Jacky regularly for dinner.

An entry on his birthday says *"Phone Dad and Nick"*, but after that the entries are few and far between.

Continental Pullman

The archive contains a formal letter written by Greg Williams dated 18 March 1988 to Transatlantic & General Securities of Chelmsford. The letterhead says Continental Pullman Holdings B.V. and the address at the bottom is Brouwers Hoek 26, Borsbeek, Antwerp, but the letter appears to have been written in England. It is the last written reference to Continental Pullman in the archives, but there is also an embossing tool that bears the name (and another one that says 'Master Find Limited').

A few days later on 23 March 1988 there is an invoice from a company named Hi-Grade Computers Ltd of Kentish Town Road showing the purchase of a brand new computer with a 44 Mb hard drive, a copy of MS-DOS 3.3, a printer with a parallel lead, and a floppy disk. Total cost including VAT was £1834.30. The invoice was made out to *"Staffbase, 99 Green Road, London N14"*, a residential property near Oakwood station in Southgate, and not very far from Winchmore Hill Road.

Greg Williams

Winchmore Hill Road

The Montrose Avenue address in Luton appears on Greg Williams' International Driving Permit, which was issued through the AA at Basingstoke on 30 January 1989.

Whether Greg ever actually lived on the premises or was just using it to receive mail is not known.

Another archive document shows that on 31 January the half-yearly distribution from Windsor Property Shares Trust was £6.82, which does not sound like a cause for celebration.

The archive also contains bank statements for Greg's business and current accounts, both of which are dated 6 June 1989. They don't look too encouraging either.

I am in no position to give an informed opinion, but the impression I got was that Greg's finances were perilous at this point - they were certainly a long way from the glory days of Magic Bus.

****

The final document in Greg Williams' archive is a CV dated 31 July 1989. There is a draft with comments that has clearly been composed on a computer, then another cleaned up version that was printed out on a dot matrix printer.

Greg used the latter to apply for a job with General Electric (USA) in Hammersmith, who were looking for a Programme Manager *"for the new business sector of Trade & Transportation"*.

"I would like to introduce myself to you", wrote Greg, *"as being ideally suited for this position"*. But he wasn't hired.

Greg's address was 229d Winchmore Hill Road, London N21.

The Final Curtain

Barrie Moreton, who wasn't present, told me he believed that Greg Williams had been sharing the Winchmore Hill Road property with a girlfriend and some of his former employees from the London office. Greg was the tenant.

On the August Bank Holiday weekend the others had apparently taken a mini-break somewhere, while Greg had stayed behind. When they returned they found that he had taken his own life.

Barrie's partner Helen Straw, who was working in London at the time, attended the inquest on 14 November, and when I met her she spoke movingly about the experience - Barrie and Helen both considered Greg a good friend and a very sad loss.

The Payoff

Greg Williams killed himself on 28 August 1989. The cause of death was an overdose of Tamazepam. The inquest heard that he had recently suffered a significant financial loss due to a major stock market crash (there had been two in succession).

What was not mentioned at the inquest was that Greg Williams had written a cheque for £25,000, put it in an envelope which he addressed and stamped, and went out to the letterbox to post it before using the self-checkout.

The cheque was sent to Jacky, and was cashed.

The Funeral

Greg Williams was cremated in Bournemouth. Nee flew over from USA, Barrie Moreton, Helen Straw and Pete Smith also attended, along with Greg's family members and others.

Rest in peace.

****

****

66 Shaftesbury Avenue, London W.1.
01 439 8471 · Telex 21194

Chapter 8
THE LEGACY

Main Offices in: London·Amsterdam·Paris·Athens

Magic Bus Legacy

Magic Bus remains indelibly associated with the Hippie Trail.

To be more accurate, it is the *idea* of Magic Bus - because very few people actually know anything about the company.

Tony Wheeler of *Lonely Planet*, who had travelled the route to Kathmandu in 1972, said that he didn't think a company even existed, and that it was just a generic term.

Rory MacLean, who wrote a book called *Magic Bus* that purported to be about the Hippie Trail, didn't even mention Greg Williams in it, choosing instead to focus on a *"cockroach-infested office on Amsterdam's Dam Square"* that never existed.

"The secret of a successful trip", according to MacLean, *"was to get the passengers smoking chillum dope pipes before breakfast"*.

I hope we can improve on that.

The Drivers

The vast majority of drivers weren't directly employed by Magic Bus, which quickly became a booking agency. Compiling a full list is likely to be impossible, so apologies to all who are missing:

Neil Stevens, Tim Hatfield, Jeff Mayer, Tony & Kathy Robinson, Chuck, Terry, Eric Abrahamsen, Graham Styles, Graham Bourne, Torkild Bangsbo Andersen, Tapani (Finland), John Moore, Brian Mears, Bob Turton, Ken Kreider, Steen Ratzeburg, Tom Lausen, David Wright, John Henderson, Alan Henderson, Brodie, Diego, Ludwig, Carrie Cuneo, Fritz Prang, Jan Landon, Johnny Webb, Gerard Wantenaar, Spacey Pete, French Gerard, Odd Boye Karlsen, John, James and Eddie Jeffries, and Barrie Moreton.

"You'll be an inspector, have no fear".

Office Staff

Another incomplete list - these are the names that I have:

Canadian Bruce, Hank Vann, Floyd Webb, Karen Versteegh, Helen Lipton, Sarah Carruthers, Mandy Oliver, Anthony Oliver, Peter Jodoin, Wendy Fellowes, Patrizia Falloci, Nick Weston, Valerie Haynes, Marisa, Dierdre, Paulette, Linda, Brodie, David Rendall, Peter Hoornweg, Maarten Bolluijt, Robert Ragir, Bernard Stolter, Jan Kuntkes, Wim Jansen, Margreet Elings, Willeke Schouten, Koos Schouten, Rodda Thomas, Phil Sutton, Michael Willemsen, Hanneke, Pierre René, Torkild Bangsbo Andersen, Kevin Buckley, Jacques Muscat, Mike Newton, Andy Kirk, Fortunato, D'arcy Paladeau, Laurence Tarot, Guenther, Madeleine, Truusie, Therese, Jan, Greet, Bernardien, Henry, Agnes, Gustaviolo and Lunaticos.

Ephemera

Greg Williams' archive contained surprisingly little in the way of Magic Bus ephemera - just a few documents and a poster from the early days plus a Magic Inn business card.

Leaflets are on display in some of the photographs, many of which seem to have been taken at the London office in the 1980s - the classic logo is highly visible on most of the printed matter. Some 1982 ads mention a *"full colour brochure"*.

There is almost nothing on the web, even in an era when relics from the past are venerated as 'iconic' - when it comes to Magic Bus it seems that nostalgia ain't what it used to be.

Those of us who were aware of Magic Bus at the time find it baffling. The company was very well-known and advertised heavily in the press, with countless thousands using it. And it was synonymous with 'the bus to India' in the public imagination, even though it was just one of many operators on the route.

I suppose that - unlike Tony Wheeler - you had to be there.

Magic Tickets

While there are no Magic Bus tickets preserved in the archive, I have seen a few photographs online of one that was issued by the Damrak office in December 1979.

The classic logo is on the front, the actual ticket details have been torn out (as in 'used'), and there is some promotional blurb:

"As far as travel is concerned MAGIC BUS has become a unique phenomenon. Our aim is to provide the cheapest possible transport whilst maintaining a high standard of reliability. Within Europe we have built up a network of bus routes which offers travellers comprehensive regular services to almost all countries and destinations. This European network augments our well-known service to Athens and Asia. We also arrange expeditions in Africa & South America. Our boat-train services have been used by over 100,000 budget-minded travellers. Our flight service offers sharp reductions on a wide range of inter-continental flights. If you are interested in further information about any of these programs please do not hesitate to call at one of our offices".

Magic Bus office addresses listed are at Damrak 87 (Amsterdam), 66 Shaftesbury Avenue (London), 28 Rue du Pont Louis-Phillippe (Paris) and 24 Kidathineon Street (Athens).

Nee told me that the Magic Bus office in Paris was run by Pierre René, and an online forum post from 'Michele' on Blogspot said she *"used to work for the company in Paris at Place de Madelaine [sic] putting students on buses to Amsterdam".*

Sales Manual

One item of ephemera that was preserved is a ring binder marked 'Sales Manual' in red with a Magic Bus logo featuring a hybrid bus and plane. There were no 'Sales Manual' contents, so it now houses Magic Bus archive documents.

Been There Done That

The first Magic Bus t-shirt that I came across was worn by an as yet unidentified guy in one of Greg's archive photographs.

It uses some of the artwork seen on business cards from Magic Bus offices in Athens and Istanbul. I assume that a batch were printed for staff, but it is also possible that they were sold to the public. Barrie Moreton unearthed a similar (but not identical) one from the Athens office that had been part of the archive.

A photograph from the London office in the 1980s shows Magic Bus t-shirts on sale at £2 each in black, white, red and light blue (small, medium and large are all available). The design used is just about discernable - and it matched the final item in the archive, which had been baffling me for a while.

It was a thick waxy paper that when held up to the light revealed a faint image of a Magic Bus logo that I hadn't seen before, but seemed to use a similar version to the 'Sales Manual' image.

After cataloguing everything else in the archive I was left with this artefact, having struggled to work out what it was, or even how to separate it from the waxy paper.

Perseverance paid off. The image reproduced here does not do it justice - not only is it full colour, but it also features metallic ink. It may be an 'iron on' item - I really have no idea - but it is exactly the same image shown in the photographs of t-shirts from the New Oxford Street office.

Sales Manual and author   *Magic Bus t-shirt #1*

*1980s Magic Bus t-shirt design
in full colour with metallic trim*

Exhibitionism

Another archive shot was clearly taken at a trade exhibition, with stand C54 assigned to 'MAGIC BUS TRAVEL CO LTD'.

There are signs promoting Magic Bus, Magic Train and Magic Plane, using variations of the classic logo, but the main focus of the display is Magic Freight - featuring a baby grand piano.

"Do you know the piano's on my foot?"

"You hum it, son, and I'll play it", as Mr Shifter would say.

Company Song

Amongst the various papers that Greg Williams preserved was an undated handwritten draft of a 'company song'.

It was written by 'Hubcap' (John Parsons) and 'Daddy Stovepipe' (Antony something illegible - a lot of Magic Bus people were given nicknames). I have no idea who they are.

> Magic bus Magic bus,
> There's nothing like it on the road,
> We've tried to do our best for you
> we only hope it showed,
> Cleaned your windows filled you up,
> + listened to your song.
> Now we're almost home + dry
> It really doesn't seem too long.
>
> John Parsons (hubcap)
> + Daddy stovepipe
> (Antony De ~~hello~~ ~~there~~)

There are several verses. Here is the chorus:

Magic Bus, Magic Bus
There's nothing like it on the road
We've tried to do our best for you
We only hope it showed

Pete Townshend has nothing to fear, I reckon.

I have actually been known to perform Pete's *Magic Bus* myself on occasion - it has nothing to do with Greg Williams or his bus company, I just happen to be a Shepherd's Bush native who grew up in the swinging sixties. And I like to *rock*.

Refuseniks

A few surviving individuals who worked for Magic Bus back in the day did not want to engage with this project - they were invited to have their say but chose not to (as is their right).

One guy who contacted me believed that Greg Williams *"contracted AIDS and died in Africa"* - but when I told him that Greg's death certificate said otherwise he decided that I was *"obviously not fit for the job"* of writing a history of Magic Bus.

Funny old world.

Kevin Buckley

Early in his memoir *The Overlanders* Graham Bourne describes his first trip to Athens as co-driver with Canadian Chuck, and his surprise at finding the front seat occupied by *"a big hairy freak, dressed in what looked like a blue bathrobe with a fancy embroidered bib around the neck"*.

"This turned out to be the Welshman Kevin Buckland", Bourne wrote, in a futile attempt to disguise his surname (which appears on the web). A six-footer with a stoop, a straggly beard, a mane of wavy ginger hair and an Indian smock, Kevin was the Magic Bus agent in Athens on his way to open up for the new season. Both Kevin and Chuck had been in Goa the previous winter.

"My job is to get passengers for Greg's buses and help make him fat", Kevin told Bourne. There was no Athens office, and Kevin would make a deal with a local hostel to run the reception desk in exchange for free accommodation for himself and the drivers.

My understanding is that Kevin quit Magic Bus in 1978 after Barrie Moreton was brought in, but continued to work in Athens with other bus operators such as Rainbow Travel.

Sadly I was unable to get him on board.

Wendy Fellowes

Wendy was reportedly a manager of the London office at some point - one of many over the years - and there is a photograph of her in the Magic Bus archive. Her partner Peter Jodoin was also said to have been a co-founder of the Magic Freight sideline.

Sadly I was unable to get her on board.

Wendy Fellowes, an office manager in London.

Pete Smith

Greg Williams was full of ideas, but any successful business needs someone who understands finance. Peter Knopper was identified as an early Magic Bus accountant, and the Belgian Gustave Girard acted for International Pullman (based in Antwerp).

Maarten Bolluijt told me that Greg's main adviser in later years was Pete Smith, who had previously worked for a company that did accounting for the London office - *"Greg took him on because he liked him and he was honest"*, Maarten said. Pete had apparently grown up in Asia and spoke fluent Japanese.

Sadly I was unable to get him on board.

Pete Smith, Magic Bus financial adviser.

Brodie

Carrie Cuneo wasn't the only woman to drive a Magic Bus.

An adventurous young New Zealander known only as Brodie had been a passenger on a bus from Kathmandu to Athens, and she co-drove a bus to India with John 'Jinks' Jeffries under contract to Magic Bus in 1977.

Brodie started work at the Magic Bus office in Athens in the summer of 1978, and in December 1979 moved to the London office, before making her way back to New Zealand in 1980.

Sadly I was unable to get her on board.

Brodie, office worker and bus driver, by Barrie Moreton.

Magic Bus advertising became increasingly sophisticated in the 1980s as the company expanded, with offices in London, Barcelona, Dublin, Munich, Paris, Athens, Copenhagen and Hamburg as well as Holland. Packages were offered through companies such as Concorde Holidays, Tracks and Top Deck Travel.

The Magic Mystery Bus

My investigations into Magic Bus began when I mentioned to my colleague Gerard Aartsen in Amsterdam that I had never seen a photograph of a vehicle with 'Magic Bus' painted on the side.

Gerard first came up with shots of the 'Circus' bus that did tours of Amsterdam in the 1970s, and he eventually found some Dutch press cuttings with photographs of Greg Williams and the original painted Magic Bus from August 1972. Copenhagen Barry then sent me his magnificent shot of the original bus in Cornwall.

Barrie Moreton gave me access to Greg's archive in January 2025, which included photographs of the original and AEC buses, and in May the shot above was sent to me by Torkild Bangsbo Andersen. My guess would be that the bus was owned and run by Magic Bus Athens at some point in the post-collapse 1980s.

My professional opinion would be that the branding is done with vinyl, and that the vehicle does not have 'Magic Bus' painted on the side at all, but that is just technical semantics.

It's still a mystery bus.

Shrinkage

In the 1970s credit cards were rare and young people were unlikely to have bank accounts. Workers would receive a paypacket on a Friday and the vast majority of purchases were made in cash.

As Magic Bus became successful there was a lot of money flowing through the offices each day. Desktop computers, point of sale software and CCTV didn't exist back then, and without rigorous systems in place some of the money left by the back door.

Barrie Moreton felt that Greg Williams was too trusting and had not put the necessary checks in place. On his first day at the London office Barrie's doubts were confirmed - two plane tickets sold, but no trace of the money (a culprit was eventually identified). The office had also run up a £2,000 phone bill, a colossal amount back then, with someone making personal international calls.

When Greg told Barrie that there were 'problems' at the London office this was what he was talking about - somewhere along the line the discrepancies would have shown up in the accounts, but by that time it was too late to do anything about them.

Brainwaves

Greg Williams wasn't a great businessman, which probably led to the company's downfall. He was more of an ideas person, and the obvious example is the branding - the Magic Bus name struck a chord with customers, so well-known that it became generic.

New routes and packages were constantly added. Barrie Moreton told me that Greg wanted to sell cheap flights to northern Greece, where a fast coach to Athens awaited, the Ryanair model before its time. Greg also championed what might be described as 'Uber for Trucks', a network for delivery vehicles that would mean they never returned empty, but the technology wasn't ready. Greg also bought a computer in 1988, well ahead of the curve.

Drugs

For some reason the Magic Bus archive contained an A4 sheet, typed on one side, giving explicit instructions on how to make Lysergic Acid Diethylamide (commonly called LSD).

Maybe Greg was given a chemistry set as a child, but a more likely explanation is that he was given the document - the early 1970s was notorious for Richard Kemp and Operation Julie (my own view is that Owsley was never equalled).

I have seen no actual evidence that Greg Williams took drugs of any kind - Graham Bourne, for example, never incriminates him directly (though cannabis smoking features frequently).

The Hippie Trail to Kathmandu, of course, was originally called the 'Hashish Trail', and Greg told the press in 1972 that *"On every trip, this bus is full of drugs from top to bottom. Customs searches at every border. They have never been able to find anything"*. The same report had passengers smoking joints - *"I see a pipe with opium being passed around"*, the journalist adds, though my immediate thought was that he had just seen a chillum for the first time.

I didn't ask any of my contributors about drugs - I have written elsewhere about my own experiences and can say with confidence that millions of other young people were doing likewise (while some used no drugs other than alcohol, or none at all).

One person did contact me to say that Greg Williams used cocaine, but this 'supergrass' was already notorious for making a false claim about Greg and can't be considered a credible source.

None of Greg's actual friends grassed him up.

I wouldn't be at all surprised if Greg Williams dabbled with drugs, but the record only shows that he got a one-year drink-driving ban in 1983. I'll take facts over hearsay every time.

Odds and Ends

The *Evening News* of 22 September 1978 had identified Anthony Oliver as *"manager of Magic Bus Tours, of Shaftesbury Avenue"* and apparently his sister also worked there. Barrie Moreton told me that Anthony had been interviewing Pete Townshend when news came in of Keith Moon's tragic death.

One promotional item says that the Magic Bus office in Paris was at 28 Rue du Pont Louis-Philippe - Torkild Bangsbo Andersen said it was run by Pierre, and a girl named Michele posted that she loaded passengers at Place de la Madeleine.

The only information I could find about the Munich office was a post by a French woman named Laurence Tarot, who had worked there *"from 1980 until the end"* and who had once done a courier trip to Athens and back.

I found nothing about the Barcelona office, though a couple of photographs in Greg's archive look like potential candidates. The Dublin office was first listed in the press as being at 7 St Andrews Street, then later in Angier Street.

In 1981 and 1982 the UK provincial press identified Magic Bus offices or agencies in Liverpool (12 Church Street), Manchester (12 Mosley Street) and Aberdeen (34 Bridge Street, actually the office of Aardvark Expeditions).

Leftovers

There is a set of 35mm negatives in Greg Williams' archive that covers a trip to South-East Asia, possibly Thailand. Many of the shots are too dark to be of any use and Greg does not appear in any of them. There is a western woman prominently featured, with an occasional western male partner. One of life's many mysteries.

Some archive photographs appear to be from Tenerife, and include two attractive young women (no mysteries there). A couple of shots show Greg in an open-topped left-hand drive American car, location unknown, there are three of some guys with guns doing target practice, and one of what may be Greg's parents.

There is a photograph of a group scene on a party boat that would need someone who was there to explain, and another of a garden party in good weather that Barrie Moreton told me was taken at Kevin Buckley's house. Peter Stephenson identified a couple in another shot as Tom and Hazel, and a few others were identified by Torkild Bangsbo Andersen and Maarten Bolluijt.

There are several other photographs in the archive showing Greg Williams with people who could not be identified. So it goes.

Birthday Card

Preserved in Greg Williams' archive there were two birthday cards: one was from Nee and the other was from a group of what seem to be employees at one of his offices, undated.

The office card has a 1981 copyright in the small print on the back so it seems likely to have been for Greg's 32nd birthday on 6 March 1982, but that is just speculation.

The full list of signatories is: *"Guenther, Madeleine, Truusie, Therese, Jan, Greet, Bernardien, Henry, Agnes, Gustaviolo, Lunaticos [sic] and all the other lunies that work for you"*.

I do like a positive vibe.

Gregory's Girls

After splitting with Nee, Greg Williams apparently had a number of girlfriends. I don't know what that number might be and I don't consider it any of my business.

There are a few old photographs in the archive that offer some potential candidates but there is no information attached, and I didn't try to investigate.

The archive contains three postcards from 1980-81 sent to Greg at Nieuwendijk from a girl named Hanneke. A few correspondents identified her photographs - apparently she worked in sales at both the Damrak 87 and Rokin 38 offices in Amsterdam.

I have been told that after the split with Nee she became Greg's 'Amsterdam girlfriend' - the notorious philanderer had another in London and possibly others elsewhere - but Hanneke declined to take part in this project, declaring it *"boring"*.

We'll just have to manage without her.

FLIGHTS to ASIA

66 Shaftesbury Avenue, London W.1.
01 439 8471 · Telex 21194

Chapter 9
THE MYTHOLOGY

Main Offices in: London·Amsterdam·Paris·Athens

Dirty Weekend

An advertisement in *The Guardian* on 20 November 1993 - posted in the *Weekend* section under 'Overseas Travel' - invited readers to phone a Bristol number to share their experiences of dreams about travel with a radio researcher.

It was headed *"Magic Bus Dirty Weekend"*.

I don't know how much response it got, or whether any programme was ever broadcast, but for me it immediately conjured up thoughts of a mini-break in Amsterdam or Paris with an enthusiastic member of the opposite sex. And some fond memories, too.

They didn't involve Magic Bus though, so I didn't call.

Some Liked It Hot

Some Liked It Hot (2000) is a coffee table book, written by Miriam Akhtar and Steve Humphries to accompany their two-part TV programme of the same name, and it features a 20-page section on *'The Hippy Trail'*.

Barrie Moreton, keeper of the Magic Bus archive, provided two unique photographs - one of the original bus painted in Pakistan and one of an AEC bus with the company name painted on the side in the style described by Graham Bourne for 'Little Bus'.

The article gets the two mixed up, classing the AEC bus as the original and the painted bus as *"another incarnation of Magic Bus"*. That's the Hippie Trail, right there.

"As the number of Brits wanting to travel east on the Magic Buses increased, services were extended to London. Tim Hunt got on board at Victoria Station in London in 1972", we are told.

If he did, it would have been the original painted bus that visited Cornwall in July and left Amsterdam for Kathmandu in August with Greg Williams driving plus 25 other passengers and a Dutch reporter on board. The service was not *"extended to London"*.

One of the photographs is captioned *"Tim Hunt (second from left) aboard the Magic Bus in 1972"*. I have a photograph from the Dutch press that shows the interior of the 1972 bus - and this is definitely not it. The error was probably the reporter's, though as Tim claims elsewhere to have had a *"really cosmic experience"* his inner calendar may have been affected.

But the fact remains that a book containing a photograph of the original Magic Bus - albeit mislabelled - was published in 2000 and is still available for purchase.

This book's cover uses the full shot.

A book that contains nothing useful about the Hippie Trail and which features the only shot of the original Magic Bus from Greg Williams' archive - but mistakenly labels it as "another incarnation of Magic Bus".

Another photograph is claimed to be "the original Magic Bus" but is actually an AEC coach that was bought later.

Cluelessness abounds.

Rory MacLean

"The Freaks' Trail to Nirvana", boasts the cover blurb of *Magic Bus* by Rory MacLean, *"has found its most enthusiastic and impressive historian yet"*. Talk about 'having a giraffe'.

Published in 2006, the book is notably light on facts. *"The original Magic Bus operated from a cockroach-infested office on Amsterdam's Dam Square"*, it says, though no such office ever existed.

Greg Williams is not even mentioned in the book, though Graham Bourne is cited in the acknowledgements. There is very little else about the Magic Bus company.

MacLean tells us that the Magic Bus carried *"students, lone voyagers and brigades of hippies to India"*, apparently unaware that the bulk of the business involved European destinations.

"Its buses were diverse and decrepit", MacLean continues, *"especially after financial troubles forced the company to subcontract. Not that hard seats and broken springs lessened the pleasure of the journey"*.

"The secret of a successful trip was to get passengers smoking chillum dope pipes before breakfast. In the early days the buses almost levitated across border posts. On their return, so much Afghan hash was stashed in their tanks that regular smokers in Europe became accustomed to the aftertaste of diesel".

It is absolute guff.

That Rory MacLean is considered by the mainstream media to be an expert on the Hippie Trail - and is the name most associated with 'Magic Bus' - is an utter disgrace. MacLean's later claim that 'hippies inspired al-Qaida' - I am not making this up - destroyed any residual credibility he may have had, and I wouldn't advise anyone to waste money on trash like his *Magic Bus* book.

Much of it appears to be fiction anyway.

A book that contains nothing useful about the Magic Bus company (and a lot of complete nonsense about the Hippie Trail).

Scott Shandler

Along The Way to Utopia by Scott Shandler was published in 2009 with the subtitle *'Traveling the Hippie Trail on the Magic Bus from Amsterdam to India'*. It covers a trip in 1975.

Shandler first heard about Europe's 'magic buses' from someone who said he might have to hitch-hike if the driver had *"utilised the chillum before breakfast"*. Echoes of Rory MacLean.

In Colorado a local travel agent who was *"very familiar with Magic Bus"* booked him on a flight to Brussels, from where he hitched to Amsterdam. He booked his Magic Bus ticket through a local agent and boarded a bus driven by Diego - it broke down and he switched to one driven by Ludwig, who eventually got him to India. The most interesting story he has to offer is of a fellow passenger doing a bizarre Frank Zappa impersonation in the Khyber Pass.

I described the book elsewhere as *"146 pages of Pooterish flannel"*, and in his conclusion Shandler tells us that *"I had inhaled the residual smoke from cannabis drug addicts aboard the Magic Bus. It was indeed a 'magical experience' crafted by a spiritual awakening in my own mind"*. Whatever paints your toenails.

Paulo Coelho

A work of fiction that has been translated into many languages is the 2018 novel *Hippie* by Brazilian writer Paulo Coelho.

The story is set in 1970. The marketing blurb on Amazon says that Coelho *"takes us on a journey back in time, from South America to Holland to Nepal, drawing on the rich experiences of his own life to relive the dreams of a generation that longs for peace"*.

The protagonist, a young Brazilian named Paulo, embarks upon *"the fabled hippie trail to Nepal"*, hooking up with a young woman named Karla for *"a trip aboard the Magic Bus that travels from Amsterdam to Istanbul and across Central Asia to Kathmandu"*.

But the Magic Bus company didn't exist at the time and the fable ends before the bus gets out of Europe. It is sometimes said that the Hippie Trail started at Istanbul, but if that is true it would mean you weren't actually on it until you left the city in an easterly direction and crossed the Bosphorus to Asia.

Much of the book consists of typically vague spiritual waffle with some sex and drugs thrown in. File under 'freaksploitation'.

Tony Wheeler

On 4 July 1972 Tony and Maureen Wheeler, soon-to-be founders of the *Lonely Planet* publishing empire, set out from London in a second-hand Mini Countryman, bound for Australia.

They sold the car in Kabul, continuing to Kathmandu on public transport, flying from Calcutta to Bangkok, then travelling down through South-East Asia, cadging a ride on a yacht to the Australian coast and eventually arriving in Sydney on Boxing Day.

"The trip that we did became known as the Hippie Trail", Tony told an interviewer in May 2020. *"But at the time we called it the Asia Overland route"*. Oh dear.

The UK media had been reporting on the Hippie Trail since 1969 and the BBC had even aired a documentary in 1970 - while the US press had dubbed it the 'Hashish Trail' in 1967.

Everyone agreed that the Hippie Trail ended in Kathmandu, even Tony Wheeler himself, who told the *New York Times* in June 2013 that it was *"the nirvana at the end of the trail"* - though in the same interview he also said that Sigi's in Kabul was on Chicken Street, a blatant howler that Wikipedia still repeats in 2025.

Tony wrote in his memoir *Once While Travelling: The Lonely Planet Story* that he'd chosen not to use *"the crammed and renegade 'Magic Buses', privately owned and often operating out of Amsterdam"* - but the original painted Magic Bus didn't set out on its first eastbound trip until August 1972 (a month after he'd left England). He does seem to have a 'magic memory' at times.

In addition to all this, in 2021 Tony responded to an email enquiry from a befuddled researcher with the classic *"I don't think there ever was a single magic bus or company or business named magic bus. I think the name was just applied to any bus heading out from Europe to India"*. The ignorance is quite remarkable.

22:00

The Magic Bus

BBC   BBC Radio 2

⏱ 57 minutes
📅 Wed 29th Jul 2015, 22:00 on BBC Radio 2

The Magic Bus tells the story of some of the thousands of people who took the Overland Trail from Europe via Istanbul, India and on to Kathmandu. Presented by Lonely Planet founder Tony Wheeler, the programme hears from some of the hippies, intrepids , freaks and travellers who set out on buses, coaches and trucks to find adventure- and themselves- along the way. We'll hear the soundtrack of those 60's and 70's experiences including the Byrds, Bob Dylan, Supertramp, Steely Dan, Joni Mitchell, Donovan and of course, the Beatles. Show less ▲

Genres
Factual
Music / Classic Pop & Rock

Source: BBC Online ❓

Some people apparently consider Tony Wheeler to be an 'expert' on the Hippie Trail, but I am not one of them.

His *Lonely Planet* company published David Tomory's oral history compendium *A Season In Heaven*, which Tony himself endorses on the cover (*"It's terrific!"*) and which is the source of many of the most enduring falsehoods on the subject: Cat Stevens writing songs in Kathmandu, Sigi's on Chicken Street in Kabul, Timothy Leary at the Amir Kabir in Teheran, Jack Kerouac's vision of travel to Nepal, all of them demonstrable nonsense.

For many years Tony was the media's first choice of Hippie Trail talking head - he actually knows almost nothing about the subject but comes across as a nice guy, and people have heard of him.

So on 29 July 2015 the BBC gave Tony an hour to enlighten us all about the Hippie Trail in a radio show called *'The Magic Bus'*, but despite my best efforts I have been unable to access a copy.

Perhaps it's just as well.

The Vanishing

Some of the Magic Bus insiders that I spoke to mentioned their bewilderment that a web search for 'Magic Bus' turned up almost nothing about the Greg Williams company.

That the results were dominated by Pete Townshend and The Who was not the problem - this would be expected and deserved. But even with references to the song filtered out there were very few results that were about the most famous bus operator to ply the Hippie Trail, a company that also carried hundreds of thousands of passengers around Europe.

Airbrushed out of history? That would imply intent, and I have seen no evidence of it. Tony Wheeler's ridiculous claim that the company didn't exist is surely lazy ignorance rather than malice. The fact is that - as with the Hippie Trail - nobody bothered to do the research, and faced with a *tabula rasa* necessity becomes the mother of invention.

In 1992 Christopher McCandless used the 'Magic Bus' name in his diary to describe the abandoned bus in Alaska in which he died of starvation. John Krakauer's book *Into The Wild*, filmed in 2007 by Sean Penn, made the story popular in USA.

In 2011 the *Daily Mail* ran an article headed *"True story behind Magic Bus trip that launched the hippy era"* - it was a plug for a film about Ken Kesey's 1964 trip. The reporter dubs the vehicle *"the legendary Magic Bus"*, though it wasn't called that at the time.

And in 2025 there is a 'Magic Bus' doing sightseeing tours of Harry Potter film locations in London - a Routemaster double-decker, painted purple, *"reminiscent of the RT-style 'KnightBus' that featured in the Prisoner of Azkaban"* (which appears to have been a triple-decker in the JK Rowling stories).

The Greg Williams company effectively vanished.

Anecdotals

Jan, the blonde who inspired me to go on the Hippie Trail, had been overland to Nepal herself in 1973 - I remember her telling me that *"everybody smokes"* on the freak buses that plied the route. She meant cannabis, obviously.

She didn't mention Magic Bus - the service had only just started and few were aware of it. Amsterdam had been known for buses to India before the company was founded, and London had been sending them since the Indiaman service began in 1957.

A web search offers many claims that Magic Bus was co-founded in 1968 by Ben Rozendal, who is said to have visited India in 1964, *"kept company with Allen Ginsberg, Bob Dylan and Ken Kesey"*, *"experienced Woodstock first hand"* and hung out with the Grateful Dead before selling his share in Magic Bus in 1970, joining the Hare Krishnas and becoming a homeopath re-named Vaikunthanath Das Kaviraj.

I can't prove he didn't, but if he did then nobody noticed.

A rather more reliable source is the investigative journalist Meirion Jones, who told me that on his return from Goa in 1976 he had bought a Magic Bus ticket to London in Istanbul.

Meirion identified the first-floor Batu Tur office in Şeftali Sokak (behind the Pudding Shop) from a photograph that I showed him - and like many Magic Bus trips in those days, the journey across Europe had not been uneventful.

"We reached the Austrian border", Meirion wrote on a web forum in September 2024, *"but the drivers were trying to smuggle in about 3 Afghan would-be guest workers & their false papers were rumbled by the guards. We were turned back & told all Austrian border posts would be notified... The bus dropped the 3 off at an illegal footpath crossing"*.

Social Media

Posts about Magic Bus appeared on numerous forums over the years, but never enough in one place to create an active community. There are some gems out there, though:

Hank Vann: *"I worked for Greg Williams during 1975/76, helped run the Magic Bus office on Rokin with Canadian Bruce"*.

Dave Moyes on Blogspot posted that he had been employed by Magic Bus as a courier on the Athens run in the 1978 and 1979 summer seasons:

"As couriers, we had deals with the hostels and bars in Athens, where we would take our passengers to stay/drink, in exchange for free bed & drinks. We would spend 3 days and nights on the road to either Paris or Amsterdam and then party like crazy for our three days off in Athens".

Sounds like a fair trade. Any more, Dave?

"I could tell you story after story about my times with MB, as the road trips were always full of adventure, romance, heartbreak, drinking, smoking hash, sleepless nights and confrontation with border guards (Always Yugoslavia)".

Other sources confirm that on the trips from London the courier would board the bus at Ostend or Zeebrugge - perhaps bringing a knowledge of foreign languages, or to ensure that the driver stuck to the advertised route and didn't drop passengers off in the middle of nowhere. But most posts from couriers are anonymous:

"What a life experience that was... worked as a courier in summer 81. Buses on fire going through the old yugoslavia and passports going up in flames, young children building the motorways, the odd dead body by the side of the road and of course the Yugo police at the border picking up 2 bottles of metaxa and 200 marlboro every time you passed. A big canadian guy in the athens office and a welsh guy..."

No names, no pack drill. Here's another courier:

"Some of the drivers were a pleasure to work with, while on the other hand there were the bastards who only cared for themselves and getting home as quickly as possible. It was not unusual for them to expect passengers to accept being dropped off on a highway on the outskirts of Thessaloniki for example. I had some of the best times ever working for Magic Bus, but there were days I felt helpless".

Other couriers were happy: *"Anything went on bus party".*

Hotel California

Up against very little competition, the Flickr Hippie Trail Group had the longest relevant thread that I could find, nominally about Hotel California in Athens.

Dave Moyes remembered the place in 1978-79, and another poster (it was apparently Christo Parthenoglou) listed Magic Bus couriers named Richard Day, Dick Palmer, Errol Waltzer, Bill Pugh, Greg Anderson and Andy Kirk.

Another poster placed Hotel California on Peta Street. Amanda Boyce said she worked there and had photographs. Andy Oliver seems to have had a great time there too. Peter 'The Sheriff' Stephenson also contributed.

"I used to do the boat tickets in the Magic Bus office in Athens" said a poster named Nikitas, who also spoke very fondly of *"Fortunato, Mike Newton, Kevin Buckley and all that pioneering mob that set up the business of Magic Bus".*

For many young people, Magic Bus was all about the summer trip to Athens and back, twenty-somethings and teenagers heading for the sunny beaches and lively bars of the Aegean and engaging in the traditional pastimes of youth (which the poet summed up as *"sex and drugs and rock and roll"*). Woohoo!

Facebook

I am not now, and have never been, a member of Facebook.

Consequently my access to the corporation's pages and groups is severely limited - most people who post are unaware that they are in a 'walled garden' and that very little of the content is available to the general public (when Facebook says that pages are 'public' they apparently mean 'available to other members').

When I click on a link what usually happens is that the page starts to load then I am told to login to continue. Useless.

The non-member's customary experience of Facebook.

On 30 March 2025 a web search unexpectedly led me to a thread started by Martin Duce, in which he stated: *"I was on the Magic Bus (the original one to India I believe) from Istanbul to india in 1971... it had wooden slatted seats, which weren't exactly comfortable, & a nightmare if you had a bad stomach".*

The year was actually 1972, and Martin boarded the bus in August. As for the company name, Martin tells us that *"It was a good one, even sung about by The Who. I think it first appeared with hippies in San Francisco. They had a magic bus".*

Oh dear. Pete Townshend didn't write a song about Greg Williams' company (or about Ken Kesey and the Merry Pranksters, whose bus was not referred to as 'magic' until much later).

But the thread was busy so I took a few screenshots.

Rodney Twiss posted to say that *"in 1972 aged 25 and with winter approaching I joined the original Magic Bus in Kabul after a fantastic month in Afghanistan"*. Heading west, he got off in Istanbul.

Jan Landon apparently drove for Magic Bus in 1975 or 1976 (it may have been both), and said of Greg Williams that *"he told me a few weeks before he died that he'd lost his curiosity for life"*.

Pete Woodall posted *"Many moons ago I sold many 'tickets' for Magic and many other buses from outside the American Express building in Athens"*, while D'arcy Paladeau added *"I worked Magic Bus Athens in the 70s and early 80s"*. At least they were relevant.

Phil Gardner responded to Martin Duce thus: *"Was on one in 72 from Amsterdam. A few of us got off in Istanbul due to bad vibes on bus went from Istanbul to Kabul with Afghan olympic weightlifting team and their wives returning from Munich Olympics. A great journey. Then on to Delhi with another bus"*.

The weightlifting event ran from 26 August to 6 September that year. Phil, like many other posters, didn't travel by Magic Bus.

Another poster followed up with *"I'm 73... first overland in '70"* - it was nothing to do with Magic Bus (which didn't exist in 1970) and there were many similar off-topic posts.

The problem with a lot of these threads is that they are filled with bragging and self-promotion, imparting nothing useful about the original topic and going off at a tangent. They only illustrate how useless Facebook groups are as a historical source

On the other hand, Paul Fraser included a mention of *"this guy Richard Gregory"* with a link to my website, and Monday Lapsong posted a link to my page on the history of Overland buses. So it wasn't all bad - but it didn't make me want to sign up.

When I tried to visit the page the next morning I was locked out, as usual, and I have been ever since. So it goes.

D'arcy Paladeau

Another Facebook group was started in 2023 by D'arcy Paladeau, who had worked for Magic Bus in Athens in the early 1980s.

This group was much more focused but largely consisted of people who knew each other, and who consequently didn't feel the need to identify those in the photographs.

Andy Kirk and Mike Newton (a Rhodesian who designed some of the Magic Bus business cards and t-shirts) appear, and so does Servet Gokkoyun. D'arcy himself is also shown.

The group was only active briefly, it seems, but had some excellent posts - there were even some Greek contributors, which is unusual but very welcome. Chris Petropoulos' second wife Ria posted, as did Magda Poupaskale Parisi (about whom I know nothing), who provided a splendid shot of a latterday Magic Bus.

As usual with Facebook my access was severely limited - I grabbed a few screenshots while I could before being locked out - and my attempts to contact Ria and D'arcy were unsuccessful.

Reunions

Predictably enough, a few reunions were held, though any details are sketchy at best. Sylvia from the Amsterdam office mentioned one scheduled for September 2010 in London, Peter Stephenson mentioned another in Amsterdam attended by Kevin Buckley and Jacques Muscat in about 2014, and Barrie Moreton told me there was one in Edmonton - Canada, not north London - with a lot of Magic Bus people present (including himself) in the 1980s.

Summer of '79

One vivid description of the Magic Bus scene that came my way was a piece by Gough Storey titled *Fear and Loathing in Amsterdam in the Summer of 1979*, an entirely believable account of youthful hedonism and debauchery in Europe.

The author enjoys the city's many attractions, hanging out at the Egg Cream, the Melkweg and the Bulldog, and describes visiting the Magic Bus office on Damrak, which *"could be easily identified by the spindly marijuana plants growing on the balcony of the first floor"*. He notes that Magic Bus was *"chiefly famous for their overland buses from London to Kabul and even Delhi"*.

Along with a member of staff who he calls 'Brin', the author boards a Magic Bus to Athens. The Greek drivers, who I will call 'Demis' and 'Roussos', smoked *hashish* all the way, with Gough and Brin prevailed upon to roll large conical joints for them in the style of the renowned Camberwell Carrot from *Withnail and I*.

"We survived the trip and eventually grew up and moved on to more serious life pursuits like careers, family and kids", Gough writes, *"but that Magic Bus trip still stands like a beacon to the reckless stupidity and self-indulgence of our long-departed youth. And, I for one, wouldn't have it any other way"*.

I spent a rather self-indulgent Xmas 1979 in Amsterdam myself, and I wouldn't have had it any other way either.

Detestimonials

In the early days Magic Bus had a poor reputation, often deservedly, and there are plenty of online posts that are critical of the service:

"Most memories were of screaming from passengers".

"Four days and nights of pure hell".

"So many nightmare journeys".

"Our bus broke down in the middle of nowhere and the passengers were told that we would be given a partial refund and left to fend for ourselves".

That is just a small selection, and there is no doubt that some Magic Bus trips were a disaster - but the majority of posters look back at their youthful *"crazy days"* through a rose-coloured prism.

Jill Williams posted my favourite observation on the Ninebattles forum: *"The bus stank of weed and we definitely felt the effects of it, my mum thought it was brilliant".*

Secret Love Child

On 22 March 2025 a Greek 'journalist' named Spiros Vasileiou posted a piece online in which he claimed - according to Google Translate - that I am the son of Greg Williams, the founder and owner of the famous Magic Bus company. I kid you not.

Assuming that Google Translate is correct, Spiros Vasileiou the Magic Bus expert is claiming that the 5-year-old Greg Williams had carnal relations with my mother, left her in the lurch, never paid a penny in child support and never once bought me a Xmas or birthday present. *Bastard!*

It was, of course, complete nonsense.

"Richard Gregory? Never heard of him!"
While it was never made explicit, I have no doubt
whatsoever that Greg Williams' choice of company name
was derived from the song by Pete Townshend.

Who Knows

Peter Dennis Blandford Townshend had to pass an audition to join Roger Daltrey's band The Detours in 1961, and when they needed a change of name in 1964 it was Pete's friend Barney who suggested that they call themselves 'The Who'.

The band already had a popular regular gig in Shepherd's Bush at the Goldhawk Social Club, near Roger's childhood home, and have been associated with the area ever since. My local heroes.

Pete wrote almost all of their original material, including the song *Magic Bus* - he first made a solo home demo in 1965 and the band recorded it as a single in 1968.

Was Pete aware of the Dolbier and Gergely children's book called *The Magic Bus* from 1948? History is silent on the matter.

A promotional shoot for the 1968 single featured the band, some 'dolly birds', a painted thespian, a macaw and a baby elephant on an old bus outside the BBC studios in Lime Grove, Shepherd's Bush - some footage also shows the vehicle driving in the West End with paper signs saying 'Magic Bus' stuck on the side.

Another promotional shoot used a psychedelically painted Midland Red double-decker - it didn't have 'Magic Bus' written on it, but a clip exists of Tony Blackburn introducing the single on TV with a toy London bus that apparently did (if you believe him).

Pete Townshend was at times dismissive of the song, considering it something of a throwaway, and it's fair to say that the lyrics are not exactly deep and meaningful. But Pete also liked to entertain, and *Magic Bus* - which he later described as *"a singalong thing"* - was a fan favourite, the encore that closed the *Live At Leeds* show.

Pete wore a white boiler suit in those days - and Greg Williams was wearing one when Nee first met him in 1971. Coincidence?

A promotional stunt by The Who from 1968.

Another promotional stunt by The Who from 1968.

66 Shaftesbury Avenue, London W.1.
01 439 8471 · Telex 21194

THE EPILOGUE

Main Offices in: London·Amsterdam·Paris·Athens

GREG WILLIAMS
1950 - 1989
Photograph by Barrie Moreton

****

Cornelia Olsen

Originally she was Cornelia Gaines, then Cornelia Williams, but these days Nee is known formally as Cornelia Olsen.

Nee had travelled on the first proper Magic Bus trip from Peshawar *via* Kabul and London to Cornwall in the spectacularly painted bus. She later *"drove a desk"* at the early offices in Amsterdam and London, a founding partner of the Magic Bus company.

This project was already well underway when Barrie Moreton dug out an old US phone number and called it for the first time in 35 years. *"Hello Barrie"*, said a familiar voice at the other end.

Without that stroke of good fortune I would not have been able to bring you the true Magic Bus origin story - not least because Greg Williams told so many false versions.

Nee kindly answered my questions by email and put me in touch with Maarten Bolluijt for an account of the company's later years. Along with other insiders they corrected my many mistakes.

Nee came to England in September 2025, and we met for the first time at a hotel in west London. Softly spoken but assured, she put me at my ease and then completely stunned me by revealing that she had personally done the signwriting on the three AEC buses that the Magic Bus company bought in 1973.

As previously noted, my investigation into Magic Bus began when I mentioned to a colleague that I had never seen a photograph of a vehicle with 'Magic Bus' painted on the side. And the reason it resonated with me was because in my working life I earned a living for many years as a freelance signwriter.

Fans of synchronicity would have had a field day. My response was to laugh and invite Nee to my house for afternoon tea the next day - and I am delighted to say that she accepted.

Afterword

I have done my best to produce an accurate history of the Magic Bus company for posterity. Make of it what you will.

Greg Williams was clearly no saint, but I have yet to meet anyone else who would qualify for such an exalted position. In the end we are all flawed - it's only human, after all.

Greg Williams wasn't really a great businessman either - his famous Magic Bus brand was briefly a roaring success, but it crashed and burned in 1982 and his later years seem to have been largely filled with bad luck and disappointment.

But the history of Magic Bus is the stuff of legend.

And I much prefer the legend to the myth.

****

Thanks

Sincere thanks to Cornelia Olsen, Barrie Moreton, Helen Straw, Copenhagen Barry, Peter Stephenson, Torkild Bangsbo Andersen, Alan Henderson, Nigel Howell, Graham Paton, Maarten Bolluijt, Rodda Thomas, Marisa and anonymous contributors for their help, to Gerard Aartsen for research in Dutch, to Carrie Cuneo, Carl Saffioti, Graham Bourne and others who left written testimony, and to all the staff at the British Library in London.

It was definitely a story worth telling.

Richard Gregory
Shepherd's Bush

Every day you'll see the dust
As I drive my baby in my
Magic Bus

An advertisement from December 1982 that focuses on cheap alcohol in the mountains of Andorra.

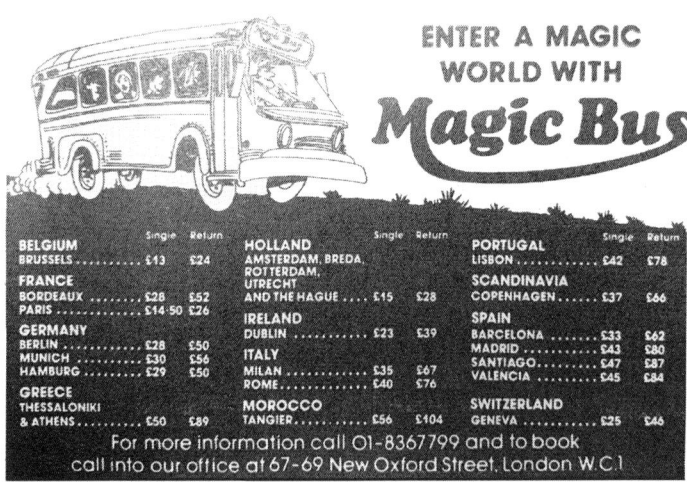

The last known Magic Bus advertisement from December 1982 with a new bus cartoon and promotions for Magic Train, Magic Plane, Magic Freight and Magic Holidays.

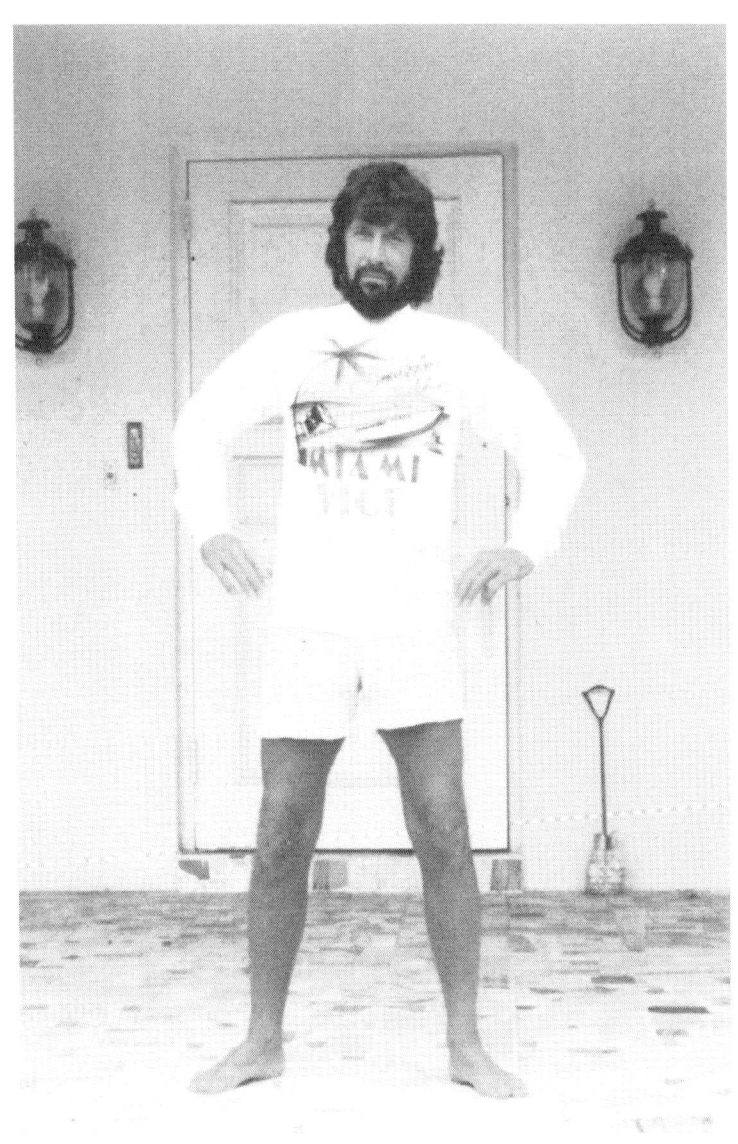

*'Obnoxious' Barrie Moreton, keeper of the Magic Bus archive,
without whom this project would not have been possible
(and who I didn't find obnoxious at all).*

From The Torkild Bangsbo Andersen Collection
Posted in online forums with provenance often unknown

Servet Gokkoyun   *Pierre René (Paris)*   *Chris Petropoulos*

*The London and Amsterdam office crews assembled
for an inter-city football match in London.
Maarten Bolluijt is lurking in Where's Wally fashion,
Dave Rendall front right. Photograph by Rodda Thomas.*

From The Greg Williams Archive Collection
Captured on camera but not necessarily identified

Who is shaking hands with Greg Williams?

Peter Knopper   *Unknown*   *Unknown*

From The Greg Williams Archive Collection
Captured on camera but not necessarily identified

Linda, Peter Jodoin and Greg Williams at the London Office.

Greg Williams and an unidentified couple in the 1980s.

From The Greg Williams Archive Collection
Apparently a photo-booth self-portrait

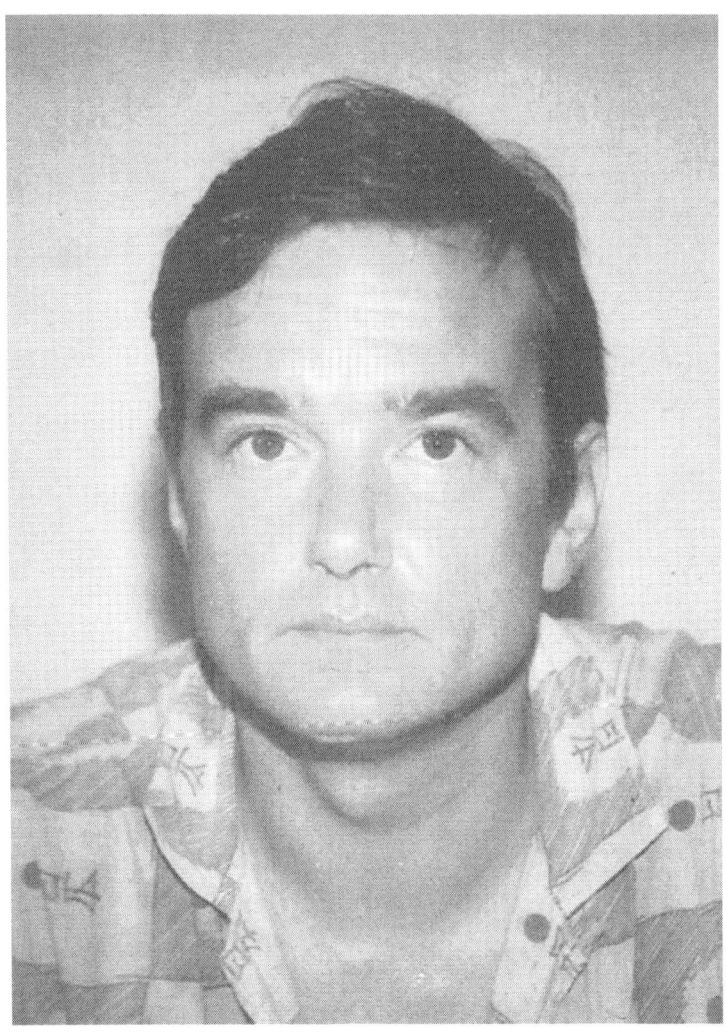

*Greg Williams passport-sized photograph.
It was used on his International Driving Permit
that was issued on 30 January 1989.*

Index

AEC Buses *28, 58-9, 192, 212*
Alan Henderson *96, 104, 106*
Amsterdam *3, 10-13, 20-29, 40-7, 50-2, 84-7, 115-23, 148, 207+*
Andy Kirk *70, 104, 165, 206*
Anthony Oliver *53, 67, 186*
Athens *26-9, 45-52, 65-71, 80, 124-6, 151, 155-6, 182-4, 202, 206*
Barrie Moreton *69-70, 78, 82, 97, 128, 150, 159-65, 168, 184+*
Beesd *11, 26-9, 32, 36, 43-7, 58*
Ben Rozendal *201*
Brodie *53, 70, 181*
Bruce Bronczyk *27, 46*
Carl Saffioti *26, 29*
Carrie Cuneo *1, 73, 78, 97*
Chris Petropoulos *69, 92, 218*
Copenhagen *78-82, 111*
Copenhagen Barry *4, 18, 47, 84*
Cornelia Gaines *12-17, 22, 26-9, 33, 47, 49-53, 59, 87-8, 104, 121, 162, 168, 173, 188, 214*
Couriers *124-5, 202-3*
D'arcy Paladeau *126, 205-6*
Dave Moyes *202-3*
David Hurd *5, 12, 15*
David Rendall *53, 128-9, 138, 147, 154-6, 212*
Duncan Campbell *111-2*
Floyd Webb *48*
Fortunato *70, 104, 203*
Gerard Aartsen *72-3, 151, 183*
Gerard Wantenaar *86, 115*
Goa *14, 65, 82, 88, 162, 165*
Gough Storey *207*
Graham Bourne *11, 32-47, 58, 62, 65, 72, 78, 84-5, 87, 117, 178*
Graham Paton *14-15*
Greg Williams *1-221*
Gustave Girard *150*
Hank Vann *202*
Helen Straw *162-3, 168*
Istanbul *72-79, 94-5, 97, 109, 111, 114, 151, 197, 201, 204-5+*
Jacques Muscat *65, 70, 104, 207*
Jan Landon *205*
Jochen Reier *47, 62-3*
John Blake *113-4, 122, 135*

ENTER A MAGICAL WORLD WITH Magic Bus

Kabul 6, 10-11, 14-15, 26, 34, 48, 85, 88-9, 107-11, 147, 198-9, 205+
Karen Versteegh 53, 103-4
Kathmandu 20-23, 26, 55, 63, 78-9, 83-85, 88, 94-5, 97, 115, 162, 171, 181, 185, 192, 197-9
Kevin Buckley 47, 65, 69-70, 80, 104, 165, 178, 187, 203
London Office 5, 47-8, 50-7, 66, 82, 92-3, 96, 103-5, 111, 114-5, 128-33, 138, 148, 154, 156
Maarten Bolluijt 50, 115-19, 135, 140, 151, 180, 187, 214, 218
Marisa 129
Martin Duce 30, 204-5
Meirion Jones 72, 201
Michael Willemsen 140-1
Mike Newton 70, 104, 203, 206
Nick Davies 145-7
Nigel Howell 124-5
Paddy Garrow-Fisher 7, 58
Paulo Coelho 197
Penny Junor 109-10
Peshawar 10-15, 22, 32-4, 214

Pete Smith 81, 168, 180
Pete Townshend 3, 53, 135, 177, 186, 200, 204, 209-11
Peter Hoornweg 52, 92, 117-8
Peter Knopper 180, 219
Peter Stephenson 65, 69-70, 84, 102, 187, 203, 207
Ray Gosling 122
Rodda Thomas 53, 121, 218
Rory MacLean 88, 106, 114, 194
Sarah Carruthers 105
Scott Shandler 196
Scottish Bob 96, 102
Servet Gokkoyun 72, 78, 218
Spacey Pete 85, 96, 102
Susan Cuneo 73, 75, 78, 97
Tenerife 164, 187
Time Out 47-8, 54-57, 67, 93, 96, 98-100, 111-2, 150, 152-4
Togo 160-1
Tony Carter 150
Tony Wheeler 1, 88, 118, 171, 198
Torkild Andersen 84, 115, 154
Wendy Fellowes 53, 129, 179

66 Shaftesbury Avenue, London W.1.
01 439 8471 · Telex 21194

THE END

——— Main Offices in: London·Amsterdam·Paris·Athens ———

The Author

A native of Shepherd's Bush in London, Richard Gregory bought a one-way bus ticket to Kathmandu in 1974 as a teenager and made his own way home using a mixture of public transport and hitch-hiking. But he never set foot on a Magic Bus.

Richard has written extensively about the Hippie Trail online over the years. His major work *A Pukka History of the Hippie Trail* is (unlike most writing on the subject) based on actual research, and is being published in book form for the first time to complement this history of the Magic Bus company.

An accomplished musician, in 2021 Richard released his epic song *Along The Hippie Trail* to coincide with a brief appearance in the fabsploitation film *The Beatles And India*.

He sometimes performs Pete Townshend's *Magic Bus* too.

Other Works by Richard Gregory

A Pukka History of the Hippie Trail

The first book on the subject worth reading, based on in-depth research and personal experience.

This unique work debunks popular myths and explains the reality as it was recorded in the contemporary media of the 1960s and 1970s.

Limited edition hardback.

All Aboard The Indiaman

The story of the first bus service from London to India, founded in 1957 by Paddy Garrow-Fisher.

Includes rare photographs from the Indiaman company archives along with personal accounts and contemporarary newspaper coverage.

Limited edition hardback.

Along The Hippie Trail

The epic biographical account of Richard Gregory's own experience on the Hippie Trail in 1974 - in song.

Digital formats only, available from streaming and download services.